W9-AXY-263

Awaking Wonder

Opening Your Child's Heart to the Beauty of Learning

SALLY CLARKSON

BETHANYHOUSE

a division of Baker Publishing Group
Minneapolis, Minnesota

© 2020 by Sally Clarkson

Published by Bethany House Publishers
11400 Hampshire Avenue South
Bloomington, Minnesota 55438
www.bethanyhouse.com

Bethany House Publishers is a division of
Baker Publishing Group, Grand Rapids, Michigan

Printed in the United States of America

All rights reserved. No part of this publication may be reproduced, stored in a retrieval system, or transmitted in any form or by any means—for example, electronic, photocopy, recording—without the prior written permission of the publisher. The only exception is brief quotations in printed reviews.

Library of Congress Cataloging-in-Publication Data

Names: Clarkson, Sally, author.
Title: Awaking wonder : opening your child's heart to the beauty of learning / by Sally Clarkson.
Description: Minneapolis, Minnesota : Bethany House Publishers, [2020]
Identifiers: LCCN 2020002039 | ISBN 9780764235887 (hardcover) | ISBN 9780764237133 (trade paper) | ISBN 9781493424924 (ebook)
Subjects: LCSH: Learning—Religious aspects—Christianity. | Imagination in children—Religious aspects—Christianity. | Curiosity in children—Religious aspects—Christianity. | Wonder in children—Religious aspects—Christianity. | Christian education—Home training.
Classification: LCC BR115.L32 C53 2020 | DDC 248.8/45—dc23
LC record available at https://lccn.loc.gov/2020002039

Unless otherwise indicated, Scripture quotations are from the New American Standard Bible® (NASB), copyright © 1960, 1962, 1963, 1968, 1971, 1972, 1973, 1975, 1977, 1995 by The Lockman Foundation. Used by permission. www.Lockman.org

Scripture quotations identified NET are from the NET Bible®, copyright © 1996–2016 by Biblical Studies Press, L.L.C. http://netbible.com. Used by permission. All rights reserved.

Scripture quotations identified NIV are from the Holy Bible, New International Version®. NIV®. Copyright © 1973, 1978, 1984, 2011 by Biblica, Inc.™ Used by permission of Zondervan. All rights reserved worldwide. www.zondervan.com. The "NIV" and "New International Version" are trademarks registered in the United States Patent and Trademark Office by Biblica, Inc.™

This book recounts events in the life of Sally Clarkson according to the author's recollection and information from the author's perspective.

Cover design by Dan Pitts
Cover art by Jamin Still

Author is represented by The Bindery.

20 21 22 23 24 25 26   7 6 5 4 3 2 1

I dedicate this book to Clay, Sarah, Joel, Nathan, and Joy,
my worthy companions in a journey of wonder and inspiration.
Who could have known how much fun, adventure,
and sweet community would come from our years of
exploring the world together?
I dearly love you all!

And to my wonderful God, who inspired us to awaken
to a different way of living and to see His miracles
and love at every turn.

Contents

A Letter to the Reader

Long before you held this book in your hands, God was writing this story on the heart of a mother. Like you, she longed to raise her children to do more than simply *survive* this world we are living in; she wanted them to *thrive*. Her hope and prayer: that each child would grow into someone who would bring light, goodness, and beauty to the world.

And that's exactly what happened.

You and I know the mother of those four children as Sally Clarkson, the beloved mentor to countless moms around the world. And now, in these pages, Sally is sharing the core philosophies that led her on the adventure of motherhood.

This is Sally's story, written in its most complete form yet. You are in for a treat.

When Sally came to us with the idea for *Awaking Wonder*, we at Bethany House Publishers offered our enthusiastic *yes!* We recognized the importance of this particular book for this particular time. In this fast-paced world, parents feel as if they are losing ground. Many are losing confidence. We hear from parents who want to raise children with healthy minds and a vibrant faith before launching them into the world. But they feel like they're doing it all wrong.

Along comes Sally to encourage and guide. She reminds us that, as parents, we cannot depend on someone else to shape the destiny of our children.

The responsibility is ours, given to us by God. "Faith, knowledge, wisdom, and moral virtue must be taught, upheld, treasured, and embraced for a lifetime. It is our service to God to be stewards of our children's lives," Sally writes.

But Sally also reminds us that we don't do this alone. God has equipped us for the task before us, and He walks with us each step of the way.

Sally's philosophy of educating—centered around a wonder-filled life—awakened something in me as I edited these pages.

You see, long before I was an editor, God was writing a story in me, too. I am a mom to two girls. From my early days of motherhood, I began to pray, "Lord, help me awaken the potential in these children. Guide me as I raise them to love you and serve you in a world that is ever changing."

As a trusted mentor, Sally has been an answer to that prayer.

The principles and philosophies in this book are tested and timeless. They will help each of us as we guide our children toward rich intellectual and spiritual growth.

Awaking Wonder is destined to become a classic as we raise up the next generation. My prayer is that this book will change the way you see the world, your child, and yourself as the chief steward of your children's lives.

When I finished reading the last page of this book, I wrote these words to Sally: "It was more of a privilege than a job to read *Awaking Wonder*, and I was thrilled that I got to be one of its first readers. You are a fine writer and thinker, with a heart so full of the love of Jesus that it spills onto every page."

Now, my friend, it's your turn. Awaken to the wonder.

Jennifer Dukes Lee
Nonfiction acquisitions editor,
Bethany House Publishers

1

A Wonderful Beginning

Wonder: (noun) "A feeling of amazement and admiration; caused by something beautiful, remarkable, or unfamiliar"[1]; desire to know something thoroughly; (verb) to feel curious and engage in imagination.

We do not want merely to *see* beauty, though, God knows, even that is bounty enough. We want something else which can hardly be put into words—to be united with the beauty we see, to pass into it, to receive it into ourselves, to bathe in it, to become part of it.

C. S. Lewis, *The Weight of Glory*

Memorable and momentous occasions rarely announce themselves ahead of time, but often tiptoe quietly into the corners of our lives and yet leave a profound influence. So this particular evening stands out to all of us as a sort of mysteriously sacred shared event that shaped a deep part of our souls.

In the late evening just after sunset, chill mountain breezes of a summer night swirled around us, and I shivered involuntarily. Thousands of stars shone above like diamonds on a velvet cloak and beckoned to us to stop, to enter into their reality.

Tonight we should sleep out under the stars, I thought. I had not seen such a cloudless, clear view of the night skies in a very long time.

When I announced my plan, excitement burst forth through squeals, jumping up and down, smiles that lit up the room. Making plans and giving orders, I bustled about, dragging sleeping bags and pillows onto our deck. At 7,300 feet in elevation, our little rustic home was tucked away at the foot of towering Colorado Rockies, bordering 25,000 acres of national forest.

We were surrounded by the long, dark shadows of the trees waltzing to a mountain song, and the pine forest whistled as the breeze gently moved branches back and forth. We found ourselves invited to a dramatic performance by an infinite array of stars twinkling across our night sky.

Here, away from the lights of the city, the whole world of sky sparkled with movement and flashes as though elegantly parading in the heavens, in sync with the pine trees. We considered that we had box seats and were audience to the angels rollicking, swirling in the light, moving to the rhythm of the swaying branches, just for our pleasure. Our magical night world was awash with mystery and whimsy.

Four-year-old Joy plopped into my lap as I eased onto our old wooden bench. Her brothers, Joel, twelve, and Nathan, ten, ran wildly up and down our deck, yelling, punching, giggling, and pointing to a shooting star here and the Milky Way there.

Clay, my husband, turned up the soft acoustic music from inside the house so that a symphony of haunting melodies accompanied this transcendent evening of delight. The night sky darkened and marked the time for us to cuddle for warmth in a pile under the sleeping bags. We all lay flat on the creaky deck, looking up into the showcase of myriad glimmering lights. In this auditorium of splendor, we all marveled. An almost sacred hush fell over us and gave calm and peace to our previously distracted souls.

Sarah, at fifteen, was wrapped in a warm quilt. Hidden in a dark corner, she watched the beauty in the safe comfort of her private imaginations.

All of us were wonder-struck at the infinite stars, the sky chandelier shimmering, the vastness of the celestial art above. A calm blanketed us in our delighted participation together as we breathed in the spectacular expanse so generously given us that never-to-be-forgotten night.

As we submitted to the silence and reveled in the glorious moment, the marvel of its vastness seemed to quell any small worries or issues that had troubled us before, and we breathed release and felt peace. Each of us was caught up in our own "mind castles," where feelings and thoughts danced through our wonderings, elegantly, freely, in celebration of the grace of our moments.

The six of us were invisibly joined together as the threads of our hearts were woven through the unspoken sharing. As we sat in reverie of the grandeur, we were enveloped with the sense of an artist greater than us, and with an awareness of being small but hidden in our Creator's magnificence. Merely to be in the vastness of such a display of power and beauty all at once was to witness sublime *reality* beyond our comprehension.

We were captured in the wonder of it all, together.

No lecture was necessary, no command for everyone to "pay attention" or to look. Our stargazing, admiration, imagination, wondering, and dreaming was a natural response to the beauty we willingly entered.

As Lewis wrote, we wanted "to be united with the beauty we see, to pass into it, to receive it into ourselves, to bathe in it, to become part of it."[2]

Wonder was already sown deeply into our psyches by the One who had made us. The drive to ponder, to imagine, to ask questions, to be curious, to ask "How? Why?" To open our hearts, hands, souls and to *know* was a part of our soul's delight.

Quiet mountain shadows wrapped us in tender arms and rocked us each in a lullaby. The stillness spoke peace. The night sky provided food for our imaginations, but each of us experienced personal, unique responses. Discoveries were already waiting to be unearthed.

Each of us had a different response and diverse thoughts because we experienced the night with unique personalities, at various ages and levels of maturity. Conformity of thinking didn't even enter my expectations. Instead, I wanted to orchestrate an evening when we would all be under the spell cast by a myriad of stars and the vast expanse of the heavens.

I hoped to awaken wonder and stir imagination as we were caught in the immediate invitation to participate. I trusted that our brains would engage without my artificial interference or interruption.

How often we miss the fingerprints of the Artist behind it all because the eyes of our heart are distracted or busy with more temporal demands, the noise of life beckoning us to follow. How different the fruit of a life given to create time for wondering, imagining, reflecting. But it must be sought intentionally; it must be fought for among the constant voices tempting us to the draw of busyness.

The Power behind a Wonder-Filled Life

Wonder is the engine that drives curiosity and propels a robust intellect.

Wonder gives us a lens through which we better view the miraculous, the sacred, the intricacy of our world around us and helps form our spiritual imagination. We ponder the personality, inspiration, and breadth of the One who crafted all the sublime natural art we behold. We respond in awe and worship.

A child fashioned by a wonder-filled life will cultivate inner strength, a confidence in his own ability to think, evaluate, and know. But those who influence children must fight to protect time for the imagination to have space to work, to have time to engage. Recognizing the elegant and complex design of human beings, we understand that each has capacity to think, to create, to acquire mental muscle, to love, having agency to act in life.

Child development experts tell us foundations often determine long-term outcomes. To give a child the gift of time to imagine, to dream, to create, to engage, and to wonder is to allow time and space for his heart to be touched by the beauty surrounding him, for his mind to have room to grow strong on the feast laid out for his imagination, and for his emotions to bathe in the tranquility of a peace-ful life in an unhurried rhythm. Then we offer a feast of theology, math, story, literature, virtue, faith, science, nature, art, music, and culture upon which to apply his wondering and wonderful mind. To lay this foundation is to give our children beauty and strength of imagination and the strong pleasure of learning and acquiring knowledge over a lifetime. Wonder is the catalyst in shaping a powerful, engaged intellect.

Wonder is the engine that drives curiosity and propels a robust intellect.

Awaking Wonder is my memoir of sorts. This is my story, my memories of how our vision for creating a "wonder-filled" life worked itself out in and through the lives of our four children, now adults, flourishing in their own lives of creativity, imagination, and wonder.

We took a different path when it came to education in our family. Over the years, I've had many opportunities to discuss the foundational ideas most important to us with other educators, parents, and, of course, our own children, who are the fruit of those efforts. We certainly employed lots of vision and ways of seeing children that guided the way we treated, nurtured, and mentored them.

It is my desire that anyone who engages in the development of children will be inspired by the principles collected here. I invite all who care about the flourishing of children, about the ability to open infinite worlds of wonder, about sparking imagination, enthusiasm, and excitement for learning to be encouraged by the legacy of a family shared in these pages.

A desire to give hope that children can be filled with delight, are able store up goodness, and can live with confidence even in the midst of challenging times is at the core of these messages. I hope this book will help teachers, parents, and anyone who works with children, and that our story might inspire and encourage parents and teachers to look at the children they influence with a new or renewed vision for how to give those children the best opportunity to flourish.

I am not seeking so much to give a formula or offer specific advice but rather to share the story of how, thirty-six years ago, my husband and I stepped out and took a risk on our belief that there was a way of raising our four children outside of the traditional 180 days of classroom education.

Longing for our children to be free to grow deeply into their capacity for learning, to expand their creative, intellectual, and spiritual potential and their excitement for diving into knowledge, we chose to educate them at home rather than sending them to a classroom. We desired that they could have space and time to access their full potential in heart, mind, soul, and body and believed that would best be done apart from a traditional school and the pathway of public education. Primarily, we wanted them to develop a passion and joy for learning and growing intellectually through the engine of wonder without the confines of comparison or competition with others.

Perhaps you picked up this book to find inspiration for how to parent in such a way that your children will be inspired, and your children attend public or private school. Keep reading! There are many ideas and principles here for shaping children in your home that are not limited by your choice of schooling. I think you will find much encouragement in this book.

Spiritual formation and cultivating a love for God and a personal relationship with Him were also central to our desire to pass on a wonder-filled life. Employing wonder in faith formation based on stories, words of truth, and tales of belief and action stepping out into the extraordinary pathways of life filled our days.

Ways to imagine the personal stories told in Scripture—and in response, to love and reach out to others amid the natural rhythms of the day—seemed a more authentic way to pass on heartfelt belief than indoctrinating our children solely with cognitive concepts of spiritual reality. Recognizing that each one is made for a relationship with their Creator, we fed their thoughts with Bible stories, theology, love, godly virtue and character, and understanding to help shape a strong basis for spiritual development. We believed this faith would emerge from a longing in their own hearts to become a part of something bigger than themselves and to become one with their Maker.

Our lives were unorthodox in our time, but we sought knowledge and learned that children raised in a wonder-filled environment could flourish in all areas of life and move into adulthood with a sense of well-being, a sense of purpose, a sense of centeredness, and a well of deep faith. Our story is about four very different children who grew up within the idealism of our philosophy and grew strong to flourish as adults.

Respect for children and their potential strength paves the way to understanding how to engage their hidden internal motivation to become strong intellectually, spiritually, and emotionally. There are many principles shared that can be applied to different kinds of parenting and educational models. Innovative ways of inspiring children to love learning are being employed in many places and in a variety of ways. My main desire is to encourage, come alongside, and inspire parents and teachers who are deeply committed to wanting to raise children with fully integrated hearts, minds, bodies, and souls.

We called our education model Whole Hearted Learning. Our desire was to create a holistic life that considered how to cultivate able minds that could synthesize ideas, thoughts, and philosophy to integrate wisdom into their lives; to cultivate warm, intimate relationships that would give emotional support and deep friendship; to give space to grow strong and vigorous bodies; to shape confidence and moral strength and character through a virtuous life; and to nurture a stable and satisfying spiritual faith.

The goal of our wonder-filled learning method was to inspire a love for learning for a lifetime by igniting the spark within each child that is waiting to be lit with inspiration, imagination, and a sense of curiosity. Believing the real person is inside the "heart," we sought to engage at the heart level of inspiration, not only the mind level of cognition. When we approach the subject of learning, especially when it comes to children, we must understand that inside each of them is an endless desire to know, to understand, to ask questions, to engage, to study and gain knowledge, to dive fully into the waters of life. We can trust they already have a capacity and drive to learn, and our responsibility is to nurture and care for this capacity.

We observe this even in babies, as in the first three years of life a child learns to speak a foreign language with a vocabulary of at least 200 words and the ability to understand more than 1,000 spoken words.[3] They learn to sit, crawl, walk, and understand nuances of emotional communication. Their brains can synthesize many complex transactions, and all of this without curriculums or formal lecturing or instruction.

We are prewired to learn, to be interested in everything around us. I read many years ago that the average four-year-old asks one hundred questions a day (as mothers of four-year-olds can attest) because learning and acquiring knowledge is a high motivation for a child. As a matter of fact, learning and accessing new knowledge is a pleasure to young children. Learning offers them a sense of a healthy, autonomous self.

For a young child, to know something and be able to share it is a sort of power—one they love to display. Pondering the whys of life and putting together abstract knowledge is enjoyable and even a hunger for most healthy children. It gives them a sense of accomplishment to learn how things work and to be able to operate more and more intelligently in their world.

I remember a day more than twenty years ago when four-year-old Joy, wearing the tattered and slightly stained pale pink ballet suit she donned each morning, ran across the sixty-foot deck that bordered the length of our mountain home. Waving bubbles through a wand over and over again for more than an hour, she smiled confidently and said, "I am putting beauty back into the mountains like God did with the stars."

If this sense of curiosity and wonder is inherent in a child, then we must believe it is also a fundamental part of our minds as adults. The ability to learn and understand, to study, to know at every age is deeply satisfying.

If we want to pass on a life of wonder, we must be engaged in the process ourselves. We were created to think and to wonder, to have time to engage in deep thoughts and profound ideas, and to have the pleasure of reading and acquiring new knowledge. To grow intellectually provides great satisfaction. In this, we were made to thrive.

Giving a gift of imagination and wonder to our children requires a certain way of living and a way of seeing our children as well as understanding our own design. It requires lots of time to feed on what is natural, away from the immediate gratification of technological devices. When we learn to honor the magnificent design of a child, acknowledging the capacity to access knowledge and ideas and to have faith and to grow in virtue already inside of them, we give them an advantage in every area of life—relationships, cognition, creativity, character, faith, and more. We become the conductors of the symphony of their life, drawing out the music of imagination that is dormant.

We do not have to tell our children how to think or what to think—they are made to learn and grow and access knowledge. What we need to do is provide them with excellent food for thought as well as superior resources, giving them personal attention, asking questions, letting them ask questions, and providing lots of interactive time. This is accomplished by supplying problems to solve, by engaging them in creative play, by filling their minds and hearts with imaginative stories that introduce them to a wide arena of their colorful world. We become their guides as we provide a smorgasbord of delightful food for their inspiration. Time to be bored so they have to learn to fill their own hours well gives them a part in owning their capacity to create, design, and quantify through the tool of wonder. But to garner this important time, we must be careful not to over-entertain or distract our children with a schedule of constant activities and commitments.

Wonder is key. Wonder fuels learning, causes a brain to grow, exercises mental muscle, and gives a child impetus to grow intellectually. Wonder is focused on the child's power to engage and influence his own world by diving fully into what is drawing him to imagine bigger and broader concepts.

Wonder teaches a child to *own* his capacity to know, understand, work, and generate interest in life.

Just as wonder is a key for children, so it is for parents. There is no exact formula for parents or teachers to follow, but instead we recognize that each of us has agency to apply our imaginations and give our imprint to education in the context of our own stories and priorities.

Entering Parenting Unprepared

Many parents come into parenthood without vision, training, or understanding of how to unearth great potential in the lives of their children. They are unaware of or oblivious to how learning or brain development takes place. They are used to trusting that the "system of education" must be the best way to serve children simply because it is the way most people have been shaped in education, year after year, for more than a century, conforming to the ideals shaped by other authorities.

This lack of training and vision causes us to be doubtful of our own untrained selves, fearing we are not adequate or capable to invest in the process of our own children's learning. We might see education as a reductive process composed of right answers, correct formulas, fill-in-the-blank norms of understanding knowledge. We believe there is only one way education happens because that is our own experience of learning.

Soul-killing, mind-numbing mobile and teaching devices

Often, smartphones and apps, computer games, and television are used to distract and passively occupy a child's time, training them to passively respond to a technological, machine-filled world without engaging the part of the brain responsible for the creation of new knowledge or unique thoughts and complex thinking skills.

Children become addicted to these media devices by a process similar to drug addiction. The immediate gratification of such passive entertainment might seem like a reasonable baby-sitter for children, and that might be the case—if the goal is to make our children easier to manage, or to pacify them so we can do what we want to with our time. But this kind of mindless activity actually stunts part of the brain and kills the unseen impulse to create. A quick online search for "effects of technology on child development" will unearth endless articles regarding this problem.

These passive ways of learning that don't engage the brain in developing mental muscle, so to speak, also destroy a part of the brain's ability to think abstractly or to synthesize and evaluate new ideas as well as concrete, practical wisdom.

When children's natural sense of wonder is spent on television, cartoons, and other media, those become the educational tools of inspiration that shape their intellect. When a child can remember dozens of movie and cartoon characters but has never read a classic children's adventure, her brain has been shaped in an inferior direction. When the toys a child owns are all characters from movies, those toys will shape her values, effectively educating her. In some ways, we become like the sources of our wonder. Disney characters become children's heroes.

Another method of education that has been employed is often ineffective in tapping into wonder. Lecture—a teacher standing in front of a class and speaking for a length of time—the method used in most classrooms as a way of passing on knowledge, is the least effective way for a child to understand a subject, causing her to lack retention of what she has heard. Only a small percentage of children are inclined to learn in this way. Classroom lecturing is the way of education most parents experienced in their own schools, and so they accept it because it is familiar.

Conversely, wonder, rather than classroom teaching, is a concept that has guided many intellects, inventors, and explorers throughout history.

Plato wrote a conversation in an ancient manuscript in which Socrates says, "Wonder is the feeling of a philosopher, and philosophy begins in wonder."[4]

Thomas Aquinas wrote, "Wonder is a kind of desire for knowledge."[5]

G. K. Chesterton commented, "The world will never starve for want of wonders; but only for want of wonder."[6]

Einstein, C. S. Lewis, Goethe, Abraham Lincoln, Emerson, Shakespeare, Fyodor Dostoyevsky, Lucy Maud Montgomery, Socrates, Thomas Edison, Lois Lowry, and so many more wrote extensively about the profound importance of wonder in the development of intellectual thinking, creating, and invention.

Wonder was the basis for discovery and creativity that transformed our understanding of the world. Galileo, Copernicus, Sir Isaac Newton, Benjamin Franklin, Edison, Mother Teresa, and Marie Curie gathered their information and developed their philosophies and theories by wondering at the natural world, using their imagination to experiment, and pursuing knowledge considered outside the box of their contemporaries' understanding. Their courage to be different in the way they imagined and studied the world led to breakthrough knowledge that transformed life.

Wonder was the tool through which Michelangelo imagined the fresco on the Sistine Chapel, the way Beethoven wrote his symphonies, the means by which Dickens wrote his novels.

Wonder leads to imagination, where we connect dots to dots in complex thought processes. The more truth we gather, the more food for thought we are fed, the more concepts we understand, the more vigorous our intellect grows. Children given time to engage the gift of wonder feel free to imagine, to dream, and to pretend. This leads them to grow in knowledge as they find the relationship of all that is swirling in their minds to the world in which they live. They are free to take time to wonder and imagine and think.

Opening Your Child's Heart, Mind, and Soul to the Beauty of Learning

Each child has individual fingerprints, unique DNA, and a distinct personality accompanied by particular preferences and drives. When a parent learns to look deeply into her child's makeup and sympathizes with his unique design, she can develop the ability to open the child's heart, to engage his mind. As the major influences in their lives, we have the opportunity to narrate forward the story of possibilities for them by speaking of their gifts, personality, skills, and potential while believing and verbalizing aloud the grand possibilities of who they are becoming.

Our student collects ideas, philosophy, facts, and stories. These synthesize and become foundations of their own mental library of the world. A multitude of stories provides patterns of truth and wisdom that contribute to their own individual expression and understanding of how to live their life. Personal motivation comes from a heart that feels free to express, explore, question, and engage in life without the pressure of a need to conform or perform for an arbitrary standard or expectation.

Parents who see beneath the surface to the heart, mind, and soul level of their children are able to listen for the fragile, innocent voice of the child's interests and drives in the direction in which they naturally long to grow strong. Inside each child is a reservoir of wonder waiting to be expressed and formed into mental strength. We accomplish this by shaping the way they are naturally made to grow, helping them fulfill their own destiny, so to speak. Inside of your child, an Einstein, Beethoven, or Bach might be waiting to emerge if given an environment in which to bloom and grow.

When individuals are unconditionally accepted and set free to live into their own abilities, skills, and passions, they are more likely to be motivated to contribute from their own natural resources. Instead of being compared with others, each child can emerge with the confidence that who they are is of great value because they bear the unique imprint of their designer, God, on their lives.

After risking raising our four children in a nonconformist lifestyle of education that valued each child's unique design, we saw vibrant adults emerge impassioned and motivated to make their own contributions to the world. Each one also emerged with an authentic faith in the God who is their heavenly Father and Creator. To honor each person within the context of their own makeup gives a sense of value and dignity, as well as confidence.

I hope that our story and this book will provide inspiration, encouragement, and practical ways to help cultivate an understanding of the power and influence of wonder, curiosity, and imagination in the formation of a child, a person. Imagine if all parents everywhere turned their hearts to understanding that the shaping of their children's hearts, minds, and souls was the best work they could ever accomplish in their lifetimes, regardless of whatever else they achieved. If personal time were valued above expedient living. If children could grow up in innocence and safety, without the threat of sexual indoctrination and values-shaping dogma from secular public opinion in their classrooms. What would children become if they didn't have peer pressure, bullying, popularity, and conformity looming in their minds?

How Did Our Own Night of Wonder Play Out in Our Days?

"Just think," I had whispered in the moment of seeing a shooting star sprinting across the darkness of our night sky, "Job tells us that when God created the world, the stars all sang. Can you imagine it? Stars singing? You can almost hear singing as you look up now into the night sky! And then in response, the angels shouted with joy, probably a lot like a crowd cheering enthusiastically at a ball game. It must have been quite the celebration."

Sarah's soft voice emerged from her hiddenness. "David wrote that the heavens are declaring the glory of God," she remembered aloud.

"Mama," quipped Joy innocently, "I want to ask God what it was like when He painted the stars gold, silver, and blue and how He decided on those colors. I want to tell Him I love what He made!" And then she snuggled closer to me and sighed with a release of the adrenaline she had carried through her little-girl day.

"I wish I could harness a shooting star and ride through the heavens," Nathan pronounced.

My imagination, alive with thoughts swirling, started working on the ideas popping into my own mind for the next morning. Light, space, infinitude of the stars, galaxies, constellations; "Let there be light."

Joel suggested, "I want to read about stars tomorrow."

"I want to draw us all lying here with the mountains and trees and Milky Way all around us," said Nathan, our relational prince.

Over the next few days, we read a book about constellations, and Joel found a video online that showed the extent of our galaxy. Nathan borrowed a telescope from a friend. Researching the Milky Way, stars, and constellations filled hours of our days. We found a book that explained and displayed the major planets, the solar system, nebulas. At our dinner table, the older three spoke with excitement and reported what they had learned while Joy colored her own picture of the night sky.

This idea led to that, and soon Galileo, Copernicus, gravity, orbiting, black holes, and comets all became subjects of research. Nightly dinner-table discussion from what Clay had found to read aloud combined with "Daddy, listen to what I learned today." We memorized Psalm 19:1–6 and heartily agreed that the heavens were indeed declaring the glory of God, and we imagined David the shepherd crafting this song from his own perch on a desert mountain while guarding sheep. Sarah and Joel composed a little poem, expressing their delight and thoughts about what had impressed them these weeks we spent in the company of the heavens.

Once again, as summer came to an end, we returned to the beauty of our deck, the silence speaking to our hearts, and submitted to the breezes blowing, the sky dancing, and the sleep that eventually enveloped us all.

Cultivating Learning as a Way of Life

The whole world was our classroom. Each day there were new discoveries and engaging encounters as we encouraged observation of the parameters of their world. As a close band of humans walking through this discovery-life together, over time we secured a deep love and connection for our small family community. Each belonged to the other and owed honor to one another as we mutually shared in discovery, adventure, and interest in life.

Wonder and Imagination as Fuel to Learning

Through engaging our children's imaginations by exposure to countless subjects, reading thousands of books, asking questions, encouraging curiosity, having them research subjects that came up along our way, we were able to cultivate ownership in a hunger and joy for learning and a deep sense of faith sprinkled through the messages of each day. Engaging them in finding out facts, acquiring knowledge, and creating projects helped them to own their interests and live into their own mental prowess as an outworking of living an unconfined life of exploration.

Many people asked me over the years, "Just tell us which curriculum you used—which for science, literature, vocabulary, history? I want to buy the best age-graded curriculum." This question was unanswerable. Some desire a formula, a reductive, exact method of how to educate children. However, each family has its own puzzle of life, and each child has a different capacity, personality, and drive. Consequently, what we did would not work in exactly the same way for another family. Education is not about enacting a prescriptive, boxed sort of curriculum-based classroom, but instead is about passing on a legacy of a love for learning, an independent joy in discovery, a motivation to bring light, beauty, and goodness back into the world of our children.

Time and space limit me from explaining what we did at every stage of life, though my husband, Clay, with my input, has already written a 375-page book with many of the details of how we educated our children called *Educating the WholeHearted Child*, which will point to the more detailed parts of our educational model. Here I am instead painting with broad brush strokes to provide an overview of what shapes a learning, wonder-full home.

Consequently, this book is the skeleton, the basics of what is essential in creating a love for learning. It is looking back and remembering what I perceived was most important to a "wonder-filled home." It is a resource I hope will help you understand the foundations of nurturing children in a humane, authentic way that best prepares them to flourish in life. But mostly it is the way *we* did it. It's an autobiography of our story of faith and risk.

To separate from the busy, conformist, activity-driven lifestyle that can exhaust children and parents alike and to move into a life of wonder requires a step of faith. Yet I hope that as I share our story, you might find permission and pleasure to apply at least some of these principles and find great joy in the wonder-filled life.

2

Committing to a Wonderful Life of Learning

Education is simply the soul of a society as it passes from one generation to another.

Attributed to G. K. Chesterton

The direction you choose to walk determines the place you will arrive. The philosophy of education you embrace will determine the outcome and consequence of your students' value for learning.

Sally Clarkson

Why a Book on Wonder, Learning, Education?

Every child is a miracle. Every single one. Each is born as a seedbed of potential for loving, thinking, creating, giving, working, and so much more. Yet they also come into the world fragile, vulnerable, and dependent on those who would care for their needs and shape their foundations for life—their physical, emotional, and mental development as well as their spiritual formation. In short, those who influence, love, and care for a child are shaping the destiny and possibilities of that child's whole life.

Every parent is a teacher. Every single one. They are the ones most closely connected to their child and who have the most personal emotional investment in seeing that their child grows healthy and strong. They have more weight in the long-term development of who their child becomes than anyone else who cares for the child. A parent's impact and teaching can be for the good or for the bad; it can shape an emotionally, intellectually, and spiritually healthy child or leave a legacy of emotional, intellectual, and spiritual abuse and neglect, or provide a combination of both of these directions. Parents are profoundly influential in the lives of their children.

Most parents deeply desire to leave a legacy of love and encouragement for their children, but sometimes they don't know how. Lack of training, pervasive secular cultural values, voices on the Internet, and pressures from work often confuse and mislead them to the destructive path of an unhealthy relationship with their child. Emotional scars, lack of support and physical help, exhaustion, bad input, and lack of leadership have confused their decisions and created havoc in their relationship with their children.

Children are totally dependent on their parents for the trajectory of their lives, regardless of the outside responsibilities that consume their parents' lives. The choices each parent makes about how they will influence their child might be determined by their prior commitments, their own upbringing, and the voices in their heads. Most often, the voice of the world invades the consciences of parents to communicate, "Let the experts do their job; they are trained to care for children."

Indeed, parents are the primary adults who *will* shape and form the way their child engages in life, relates to others, cultivates values and character, understands faith or a lack thereof, and steps into the world in either a positive or a negative way. The ways a parent influences and shapes the moments of a child's life last their whole lifetime.

What to Expect from This Book

The journey of educating my children differently has probably been the most profound legacy of my life.

Every parent has a different story, a different puzzle of life reflecting a variety of demands. Often parents must work many hours or be away from home, and the pressures of their responsibilities spread them thin indeed. However, the principles of opening the world of wonder to children can be enacted in many differing scenarios. Making time and space for rhythms of life that include exploring a wonder-filled world can be done according to the needs of each family.

Because there are an infinite number of personalities and as many people with differing ideals, there are many places and philosophies of education that are shaping children in creative and wonderful ways. A variety of cottage schools, private schools, and public schools are innovating some of the principles I am writing about, cultivating ingenious ways of learning in many differing settings. I do not presume ours is the only good way to create an environment where a great education is formed, though I know from experience that education primarily taking place at home can be a wonderful choice wherein parents and children can thrive together.

An Introduction to Our Four Children

Introducing you to our four children might give you some context for why my husband and I are passionate about sharing our story and why we hope to encourage others who feel drawn to this path of wonder.

Sarah, midthirties, is the oldest of our children. She is a mother and writer living in the south of England. She's the author of five books, with another soon to be published exploring the intersection of beauty, suffering, and faith. She graduated from Oxford University with an MSt in theology and has many devoted followers who bask in her transcendent, beautiful writing on her blog, in her newsletters, and in her books and articles. She lives with her husband, Thomas, and their two children, Lilian and Samuel.

Joel, early thirties, is completing a PhD in theology and music at the University of St. Andrews in Scotland. He graduated from Berklee College of Music and has composed music for film, the concert hall, and the church. In addition to his musical ventures, Joel is the beloved narrator of THE GREEN EMBER audiobooks and has written several books of Christian nonfiction. He has a passion for helping people practice their faith through the world of their senses and hopes to use his doctorate to better understand the way music helps us participate in God's goodness in worship.

Nathan is my larger-than-life third child, like me. He loves stories and lives his life as an actor in film and on TV, is a filmmaker of popular movies (seen on Netflix), and is also an author. His latest book, *Good Man*, explores who men were created to be by God. Together we wrote a book called *Different: The Story of an Outside-the-Box Kid and the Mom Who Loved Him*. He lives between New York City and Los Angeles, always in search of the next great story!

Joy, midtwenties, is finishing her PhD in theology at St. Andrews. She hosts a popular podcast on contemporary and classical arts that both inspires and educates her audience through her words, her music, and her life. Lecturing and teaching at the college level, running a leadership forum for graduate students, contributing articles to magazines, and authoring books and periodicals occupies her time. She speaks at conferences and writes and performs original music in her band with Joel, Two Benedictions.

My children are a gift to me that I never knew to ask for. By grace, and in spite of our many inconsistencies along the way, they have each embraced a deep faith in God, they still love us, and we all enjoy the community of family. Though we live all over the world, we are one another's best friends and gather together as often as possible. All are pursuing focused, deeply intentional, and purposeful lives within their own unique personalities and giftings.

Clay and I are very normal people, have lived flawed lives, and do not have exceptional training to qualify us as parents of exceptional children. Nor do my children think their lives are very outside the norm. Yet, creating a "wonder-filled" home and holding to the ideals I mentioned gave them space to grow into their potential and confidence to pursue dreams and pathways unique to their personalities, drives, and skills.

Planting healthy seeds in rich soil, watering them, providing sunshine, protecting them from storms and predators, and fertilizing them usually produces a healthy harvest when we are cultivating a garden. Similarly, planting good intellectual seeds, sowing seeds of spiritual formation, and then caring for them by providing the sunshine of love, watering with intentionality and character training, protecting from culturally destructive influences, and fertilizing with opportunities and relationships causes them to grow. In other words, this kind of flourishing is something that can happen in any family who cooperates with the intrinsic growth and nurturing process of human beings.

People were made to grow and flourish. We think all parents, teachers, and other adults are capable of seeing children flourish when they are cared for with wisdom.

Living by faith and seeking a different way of raising our children has, by God's grace, given our children the best opportunity to be fruitful in their adult lives. We feel quite humbled to be the parents of our children, who truly became our best friends through the journey together.

Naturally, there were bumps and storms in our pathway, but we forged through the years with grace, steadfastness, and faith for one day at a time.

Of course, we recognize there are many factors that affect the outcome of children's training and education. Each has agency to accept or reject the training and love they might have received. But the point all parents should know is that children were designed with the possibility to grow and to become healthy and strong, when cultivated carefully.

We never made it a goal to cultivate "successful" adults who produced books, movies, and podcasts or who pursued academic degrees in fine universities. That was an organic yet surprising result of what they pursued after being intentionally planted and nourished in their lives in our home. We consider their real success to be that they were so patient with us as imperfect parents and still want to be our companions—and that they chose to embrace the life and faith provided through our home.

Why People Want to Read and Know Our Story

A love for being an educator grew over time, and now it has been a passion of mine for many years. It was in the process of teaching others how to think, explore knowledge, create messages, and gain an independent vision for their lives that I began to become educated myself.

This was especially true in taking on the responsibility of educating our children. In assuming the responsibility to mentor and teach them and others, I grew personally strong in the direction of what I believed and taught.

Children were designed with the possibility to grow and to become healthy and strong, when cultivated carefully.

At university, I studied literature and speech communications. My third major was in secondary education, but that created more questions than it gave answers. Some of my idealism and practical application of learning principles were created out of my desire to move beyond the prescriptive nature of what I had learned in college. After reading, pondering, and praying, I moved forward in creating what I thought and hoped would be effective to inspire my own students.

How This Book Came to Be

About a year ago, I was asked to speak at a home education conference, which I had not done for years. I prepared a short talk about the educational process I used with my own children.

I realized as I prepared for that talk that I had spent a lifetime educating, and yet I had neglected writing a book about it. Many people had become familiar with my children within their own spheres of influence because they were having an impact through their professions. People had connected the dots, discovering that they were all related and all educated in our home. Now, some had heard more details of our story. That day, after my talk, as people waited in line to speak with me for several hours, I answered many of the same questions I have received over the years— hundreds of letters, emails, and messages from people all over the world asking, "How did you do it?" "How did you pass on a love for learning?" "What is the secret to preparing children to go into the world strong?"

And so it seemed time to put my heart for education and our family's story all in one place for others to read. What I want to emphasize right from the start is that our goal was what we call Whole Hearted Education. We wanted our children to be free to explore, while shaping their intellectual palate on the best feast of good brain food, including exposure to the best artists, writers, and musicians we could find. We wanted to introduce them to the best of books, the most fascinating history, and exploration of the beauty of the natural world. We desired to give specific training in the areas of interest that would enhance their individual lives and give them a love of and interest in learning independently for the rest of their lives.

As pioneers in home education with nothing to compare our experience to, we often struggled and wondered if we were doing enough or if we were succeeding in reaching the heart of each child. All parents feel this way.

We hope our story will give you a vision for *what is possible* in the confines of a normal home. As do all children, mine created high levels of stress. They wanted to eat real food every day fairly often, and to wear reasonably clean clothes, and they had a constant need for attention. We lived very normal daily lives with the constraints that all parents feel raising four children, which created tension and strain as it would in any family. Our ultimate desire, that our children be prepared to live a faithful story in their lifetime, kept us moving forward. These simple goals drove everything we did.

Wonderful Education Happens over Time

True principles that cause children to grow healthy and strong can be used with many different applications and in many differing environments, whether private, public, or home education. The principles we chose to follow are universal and have worked in all generations in many cultures.

The direction you choose to walk determines the place you will arrive. The philosophy of education you embrace will determine the outcome and consequence of your students' value for learning and life.

This is our story, not an academic pursuit of all the research surrounding the education of children; it is the pathway my husband and I pursued. Often, people are a bit over-awed by tests and tend to want to measure their children by the results of their tests compared with those of others. We chose to educate our children at home so that we could take them away from the prescriptive methods, choosing instead a very different way than most children experience.

I know many people would like for me to write a book of formulas—if you just follow these ten rules, or use this certain curriculum, you will be able to ensure that your children are well educated. But if I did that, it would not be true to the way we chose to educate our children. *Teaching and inspiring children is an organic process that takes each child or family into consideration for their unique skills, abilities, vision for life, and capacity.*

Considering that every teacher has a personality, a unique personal story, and different training, we must come to understand that we have great agency and scope for applying principles of teaching and shaping children in a wide variety of situations. In other words, trust yourself and your story to be adequate to inspire and create a love for learning in your home within the limits of your preferences, your circumstances, and your ideals. Don't be overly concerned with your ability, lack of training, or understanding. We grew over time, and we are still growing and learning.

May I encourage those who are new to this commitment and struggling with the lifestyle, the immaturity of young children, and the learning curve of finding rhythms and balance: Be patient, as healthy growth is slow growth. Enjoy the days, accept the limitations of young children, and trust that they will grow little by little.

Don't create too much pressure for your young children out of a desire to do well. It takes years to provide a foundation for education, and the early years are for exploring, wiggling, playing, pretending, and growing bit by bit. You have many years to grow toward this ideal. Too much pressure destroys the desire to engage or learn in both parent and child.

If you feel you have wasted some of the years of your children's lives without a good philosophy, take a deep breath and start now. Cultivating good relationships and giving a smorgasbord of great mind and soul food is good at any age.

Why Did We Pursue This Wonder-Filled Philosophy?

One last component that might help you understand this book would be to know my own background and the reason I wanted to do something different with my children.

As I reflect on my own education, I realize that I loved the friends I had at school, but over time, I became bored, restless, and distracted, and I was impatient listening to lectures day after day. I talked too much, asked questions, and had a hard time accepting an answer from the teacher's instruction as truth. Even my mother often said, "Why do you ask so many questions? Why can't you just sit still and listen like the other kids?" Eventually, I *did* learn to sit still and be quiet, but I remember mostly being very bored in school and was always relieved when the day came to an end.

It was years later, after I had completed my college degree, that I realized that my hunger to learn and understand more was a gift.

Clay and I were working in Vienna, Austria, as staff at an international, English-speaking church. We often had thirty to forty nationalities attending each week because of the presence of a United Nations community. Hosting a luncheon at our home after church one Sunday, I found myself surrounded by a couple working in Russia, an opera singer, a man who played in the Vienna Philharmonic, a couple from South Africa who were attachés at the embassy, a refugee from Iraq, and a few other friends from around the world.

As we conversed over our simple meal, I began to realize that inside of me was bubbling up a deep desire to know and understand more about the world, to be better educated. My friends were speaking of artists and musicians, books they were reading, historical events, and international politics and world issues about which I felt uninformed.

I understood I had made it through school but never truly had my imagination engaged in learning. I longed to know more, to understand philosophies, history, cultures, great books, and people. Having been bored throughout many of my years of education, never having my appetite for learning cultivated, I realized I wanted to provide a different atmosphere for learning for my children. I had no idea what this would be, but I intuitively knew I was made for more than I had experienced. I wanted my children (and I was only pregnant with my first child at the time!) to enjoy the process and to be inspired to explore and truly learn. The desire to provide an atmosphere in which wondering about ideas, digging deep into a variety of subjects, and being allowed to express individual personality began to shape my imagination.

Clay had much the same story. He had graduated from college with mediocre interest in studying. It wasn't until he was in his early thirties in seminary that he began to love education. He was also intrigued and wondered about the possibilities with me.

Four Basic Goals

The following goals began to emerge as the underpinnings of our philosophy of education in our home.

Love of learning

Make it a goal to give your child an environment in which they can be curious about ideas, stories, and people. Provide an atmosphere that respects their unique personalities and drives. Offer a buffet of subjects and experiences that will engage them in thinking, evaluating, discussing, interacting, and shaping their own love for learning and growing intellectually. An education that requires personal participation and pondering was at the heart of our learning model.

Unconditional love and acceptance

The second goal was to provide my children a foundation of unconditional love and deep acceptance for them as human beings with unique personalities, drives, skills, and abilities.

As a child, I often felt "too much" because of my big questions and an extroverted sense of adventure. I tried to engage in some subjects, but I enjoyed my friends and adventuring through life outside the classroom the most. I just stuffed my larger-than-life personality away when I was at school. I couldn't wait to graduate from formal schooling and have the chance to explore the world and find my way in life.

Consequently, I desired to create an atmosphere for my children where there would be as little as possible comparison or motivation by guilt, unnatural conformity, or performance. Desiring for our children to live into their unique personalities, I knew they would need affirmation and freedom at home to cultivate their personalities and skills. And I wanted them to feel deeply loved and personally validated just as they were.

Authentic faith and deeply ingrained virtue

This became a third goal. I grew into adulthood in the revolutionary times of the late '60s and early '70s. These were the years of the Vietnam War, the civil rights movement, the assassinations of Martin Luther King, Jr. and Bobby Kennedy, the rise of feminism, and the genesis of pro-abortion legislation. It was a turbulent time.

Consequently, in high school, even though I had been raised attending church, I began to have deep doubts about my faith. I pondered, *If someone really knew the God who created all human beings, wouldn't they be more accepting of all people and cultures, as Jesus was? If they understood God created the galaxies and seasons and snowflakes and puppies, and the ability to think, to create, to influence, wouldn't their lives reflect more of this understanding of His grandeur? If they had really interacted with Him, wouldn't their lives be different, better, more filled with light and life?*

It seemed to know such a God would change people; that it would make them different, better, more loving, exhibiting a more virtuous character. Yet most of the Christians I knew personally lived pretty much the same sort of lives as those who had no faith, and they were not exceptional in character, conversation, or life. I asked many people direct questions about what impact their religion and faith had on their personal lives, yet I never found satisfying answers to my deep doubts.

In college, I was confronted with the person of Christ in a more embodied way. I understood His intentionality to love and redeem our brokenness and to provide us with deeply meaningful lives. Being introduced to more thoughtful theology, I embraced His willingness to be present with me, to show me His life through many dimensions—through His creation, His stories, intellectually, and through His deep and compassionate love.

> *I wanted to embody an authentic faith in a personal God, the artist, the lover, the holy one— one beyond our ability to quantify.*

As a result of my past, I desired that our children not be confined to a reductive faith that was based merely on moralism, rules of behavior, pedantic philosophy. Instead, I wanted to embody an authentic faith in a personal God, the artist, the lover, the holy one—one beyond our ability to quantify. I wanted them to grow up in the oxygen of His reality embodied through all the moments of our lives. I hoped, as a result, they would grow into His very character as children who imitate their parents out of love, not guilt.

Purposeful lives

I came to believe one of the biggest motivators in all of our lives is to know our lives have significance and how we live matters. Each of us has a capacity to bring light, goodness, beauty, creativity, and love to our world. Self-actualization is at the core of this goal, believing that we matter and that our lives have meaning to keep us going forward in our ideals.

This Child Was Born . . .

Probably many reading this book will wonder if they are qualified to really teach their children everything they need to know to be able to flourish in the big wide world as adults. I want to assure you, I was not prepared or trained to be a mother. I entered into the process without any knowledge, inexperienced and ill-prepared for how much my life was about to change.

I had never baby-sat, had not deeply read about children or been interested in them, had never changed a diaper, and did not have any opinions or even a basic understanding of how to love, train, provide for, or educate children. I had been a single, professional woman for ten years and deeply enjoyed my life.

I remember the night I was in the hospital for the birth of my first child. Exhausted to my toes, shaking uncontrollably, with sweat rolling down my face, puzzlement filled my mind as I attempted to center my feelings and thoughts, to make sense of what had just happened. I never expected the birthing of a human being into the world to be so utterly draining or deeply miraculous as I held my own real-life human being in my arms.

My infant entered the world gasping and struggling to find breath in order to stay alive. The frazzled nurse whisked my little girl away to give her oxygen and find a means to empty her throat and lungs, which had filled from her being lodged in the birth canal for hours.

Within the hour, she was returned to my ready arms, wrapped tightly in a pink flannel blanket, and very quietly and calmly she looked up into my face with alert, eager blue eyes. As I held her for the first time, I felt as though God whispered to me, "This little Sarah is a gift from me to you.

Will you take responsibility for her well-being for my sake? I am trusting you to shepherd her life. She will believe in my love because of your speaking love and holding her in your arms and modeling commitment to her every day. She has a mind that you have the opportunity to shape by stretching her intellect. She has a will that will learn to cherish virtues by watching you live a life of integrity. Her faith will be formed by the truths you teach her and the faith you embody every day in your words, actions, and demeanor. In short, you will be her teacher."

God's way of providing for earthly children is to entrust them into the hands of His own beloved creatures, their parents. I realized that a part of my being faithful to God was being faithful to steward the lives of the children He gave to me as a blessing. This entrustment came to be a part of my living relationship with Him. This was the way He determined children would be cared for, by the parents who conceived them.

These are the myriad thoughts that filled my understanding as I held my little one close and pondered the mystery of being her mother. I knew I was holding eternity in my arms, that her life would have implications forever, depending on what she believed, how she chose to invest the years of her life, whom and how she learned to love.

Surprised by all of these unfamiliar thoughts, I knew that I was trusted to be the one who would direct the days of her life in a meaningful way.

Fast-forward thirty-six years, to this present moment. Three more children became a part of our little Clarkson community, and each of them was invited into the same ideals that had been brewing over the years.

And these ideals are what I will flesh out in the pages ahead. My desire is that you will find hope, inspiration, encouragement, and practical help as you ponder how best to give your own children the gift of wonder and the skills to engage fully in life.

3

A Wonder-Filled Mentor

Mentor: A trusted counselor or guide who maximizes human potential.

A pupil is not above his teacher; but everyone, after he has been fully trained, will be like his teacher.

Luke 6:40

One of the greatest values of mentors is the ability to see ahead what others cannot see and to help them navigate a course to their destination.

John C. Maxwell, *For Everything You Gain, You Give Up Something*

Mentor: A Trusted Counselor or Guide

Squished as close to me as possible on my overstuffed recliner, my young son was giving me a childish philosophical discourse about what he had been *thinking* about when he was creating a little figurine of a child outside a cabin with his play dough.

"You know, Mama, when I grow up, I think I will have a home just like this. And I'll build you and Daddy a house next door so you can be with me and my kids. We will live in the mountains. We will read great stories, play music all the time, eat great meals, talk about everything, and build a swing set outside, and be great friends. Mama, when I grow up, *I want to be just like you and Daddy. I want us all to be best friends forever.*"

This is the child who, when the mailman dropped off a package, ran after him and called out, "Good-bye, Mr. Postman! We love you."

Children come into the world with wide-eyed innocence accompanied by their uncomplicated willingness to trust and believe us and to be vulnerable without the thought of being hurt by us, their parents. They are open to a world of wonder and learn from every moment of their saturation in the world around them. My son's little-boy affection and sincerity touched a deep place inside. I knew he was trying to articulate in words something that he felt deeply. But it reminded me again that I, his role model and a steward of his well-being, wanted to be worthy of his love, admiration, and affection and needed to respond gently and be worthy of his trust.

Becoming an Intentional Role Model: Passing On Our Life

That day, he reminded me education is about relationship, about being worthy of the hope of our children. Taking seriously the stewardship of their trust as we guide them should be an underlying motivation of our hearts as we commit to influencing them. We are passing on a life, not just information.

This passing on of an inspired life begins with a mentoring mentality, the idea that inspiration and understanding develop best from a thriving relationship with the one who guides the wonder and learning.

I think this concept is essential and foundational to cultivating a love for learning, a curious exploration of the world, a diving into ideas, thoughts, and discovery in life. More traditional concepts will follow, but if you miss the concepts in this and the next chapter, you will miss the basis from which long-term influence emerges and grows.

Learning, growing in curiosity, pondering ideas, and creating new thoughts are not dependent primarily on academic studies or finding the right curriculum. It is not only about teaching every fact or subject our students need to know. Instead, it is about an organic lifestyle that synthesizes family, home, classroom, and life and honors the human beings we serve. This means our plans will be constantly changing; we will grow and be stretched, developing lifegiving goals in the scope of our moments.

Clothing ourselves with an understanding of what a mentor is gives us heart motivation for the external activities that will take place over years. Teaching or influencing is a process, not a formula for one size fits all, every year the same.

Mentoring well is about passing on a love for and a vision of all that encompasses the truth and the best in life: values, faith, relationship, knowledge, character, purpose, world view, family formation, philosophy, service of others, manners, life skills, and so much more.

What a responsibility we have to fulfill in the lives of our children, who look to us to find out about life. "I want to become just like you" bears such importance.

Becoming a Worthy Mentor: The Starting Point of Teaching

From the beginning of time, men and women have had the insight to learn from those who came before them. Socrates mentored Plato. Plato mentored Aristotle. C. S. Lewis and J. R. R. Tolkien co-mentored one another by meeting each week for many years. Anne Sullivan mentored Helen Keller.

The heart of a mentor is to act in relationship for the benefit, development, and well-being of the student. A worthy mentor seeks to maximize the human potential of the one being influenced. Even Solomon wrote about it: "He who walks with wise men will be wise, but the companion of fools will suffer harm" (Proverbs 13:20).

Jesus talked to His disciples about it:

> A pupil is not above his teacher; but everyone, after he has been fully trained, will be like his teacher.
>
> Luke 6:40

The ultimate mentor was Jesus, who lived the reality of what He wanted His disciples, His students, to become. Jesus emphasized this principle when He said the student would become like his teacher. In other words, what the teacher believes, teaches, and models is what the student will become. As a model for us in mentoring, Jesus lived among His disciples, taught them every hour of the day, ate with them, modeled love and righteous living, served them, washed their feet. His desire to pass on the kingdom vision for life meant that He was "all in" with His disciples as the servant leader. His heart was to model and live out what He wanted them to become. And so they did, after He died.

As a model for us in mentoring, Jesus lived among His disciples, taught them every hour of the day, ate with them, modeled love and righteous living, served them, washed their feet.

Can you imagine how different Christianity would be if the disciples had just been given a book to read and to be tested on at the end of the reading instead of having a personal, in-the-flesh, loving mentor-friend? This begs the questions for us: Are we the people we want our students to become? If your student becomes like you, what will he be like? What would we need to change to be the model of what we hope to nurture them to become?

Words that describe the role a mentor plays might be *coach*, *cheerleader*, *trainer*, *instructor*, *director*, *guide*, *inspirer*, *friend*. All of these images offer us an example of what role we, as parents or teachers, might play in the lives of our children. As mentors, we become role models.

Parents who choose to mentor their children actively initiate relationally toward them and seek their overall well-being and long-term development. It is a lifelong relationship that is active, intentional, lifegiving, and responsive. It is not so much about merely passing on knowledge, but inspiring to possibilities, drawing out skills, casting vision, and engaging the student's mind and heart in imagining and envisioning their own personal potential. Mentors do not just disseminate facts, they embody a force of life, love, and inspiration. They become personal in their relationship to their "students."

Cultivating a relationship with this in mind depends on the active and intentional relationship the teacher has with her student. And yes, it costs time, patience, direct involvement, and focused encouragement, understanding, and growth over time. The outcome of being influenced by a personal mentor who is also growing is radically different from that of a child who is required to cover amounts of material presented by multiple teachers in classes of many students. Individual attention goes deep and lasts for a lifetime.

Cultivating My Own Heart and Soul

I realized that shaping my children called me to become my best self. It required me to grow, to be an active learner, to be enthusiastic about the subjects we studied. When I treasure loveliness of values, greatness of thoughts, civility of life, and honor in my treatment of others, people who come into contact with me will draw from the beauty I have invested there.

In taking responsibility for influencing my children's lives, I had to make goals of growth and maturity for my personal life. My passing on a legacy of wisdom meant I had to be seeking and storing up wisdom for myself. If

I wanted to pass on faith in God, I had to grow in faith through my own systematic reading, studying, praying, and engaging in faith every day. Then I was more able to embody authentically what I hoped they would learn, digest, and adopt as their own values, thoughts, and behavior.

Children draw out of what already lives inside the one who is influencing them. Consequently, as a parent I understand that I must embody what I want my child to cultivate. As my child watches and observes my attitudes, my values, my words, and my behavior, he will ingest what he imagines and understands and then emulate it. Embracing a mentoring philosophy automatically requires more investment and attention of the parent.

Interesting to me was the fact that this model for parents influencing their children was the very way God instructed parents to teach their children hundreds of years before Christ, when God gave the law to His people in Deuteronomy. It is written,

> "Hear, O Israel! The Lord is our God, the Lord is one! You shall love the Lord your God with all your heart and with all your soul and with all your might. These words, which I am commanding you today, shall be on your heart. You shall teach them diligently to your sons and shall talk of them when you sit in your house and when you walk by the way and when you lie down and when you rise up. You shall bind them as a sign on your hand and they shall be as frontals on your forehead. You shall write them on the doorposts of your house and on your gates."
>
> Deuteronomy 6:4–9

Three parts emerge:

1. He required that parents love the Lord with heart, soul, and might first of all. He wanted parents to commit to this first.
2. Then He admonished that these words of His commandments were to be on the hearts of the parents. In other words, they were to ponder, understand, honor, engage in loving God actively, at the front of their thoughts, at the center of all they valued.

3. From this life of wondering, imagining theology, this well of wisdom and understanding that daily lived inside of them, they were to draw in teaching their children diligently, when at home, when walking, when lying down, when rising up; it was to be on their minds and hearts at all times.

In other words, the parents were to be the ones who embraced a love for God, then stored up wisdom, and finally, in a very natural path of life shared with their children, they were to teach, converse, pass on, discuss all the hours of the day from the life of their own ponderings.

Mentoring as a way of teaching was the approach of parents influencing their children from the beginning of biblical wisdom thousands of years ago.

Embodying What You Want to Inspire

Iron sharpens iron,
So one man sharpens another.

Proverbs 27:17

The role of a teacher became the first focal point of our philosophy. Since as far back as Plato's time, it has been written that education was not so much about filling a bucket (opening the brain and pouring in every possible fact and academic knowledge), but about lighting a fire—true teachers being those who sparked a fire of motivation in the hearts, minds, and souls of their students to love the process of knowing and learning. Our goal as mentors is to draw out our children's internal ability to think, to create, to engage in possibilities, to engineer original ideas; then our focus must be to ask questions, to draw out the ideas that are percolating inside of the mind and imagination of our student.

In short, lighting a fire of imagination, vision, excitement for learning is the goal of our instruction. We facilitate the development of mental muscle by giving the child practice in evaluating, coming up with solutions to problems, and asking questions or pushing against the information we present in order to better understand what we are teaching.

Wrong or incorrect answers are a part of the process of learning to think truly. We challenge their answers by asking, "Have you considered this?" Or, "How would you implement that?" We lead them in the direction of logical thinking and insight as a process. Education is a journey in a direction, not an exact, premeasured step.

> *The teacher or mentor is the first and most profound determiner of how a child will grow in the love of learning and in creative freedom to explore and question life and discover answers.*

Consequently, the beginning and some of the most profound factors of my own understanding of education did not focus on grades, curriculums, tests, or behavior. The teacher or mentor is the most important asset in lighting a fire, becoming a guide who inspires wonder, imagination, and learning. The teacher or mentor is the first and most profound determiner of how a child will grow in the love of learning and in creative freedom to explore and question life and discover answers.

Replacing the Old Voices with New Understanding

Providing a different way of education required me to evaluate my own experience of education as a child. I asked friends, teachers, and colleagues how they would describe school and the classroom as they knew or experienced it. These were the generalizations I heard.

Describing education or classrooms brought to mind children sitting still, all in rows at desks with textbooks open, a teacher lecturing at the front. The teacher usually asked for the "right answer" to the questions posed, or for the student to follow a multiple-choice, fill-in-the-blank model.

Evaluating curriculums or textbooks was the method for covering the material in most classes. Every page of a textbook was somehow considered to be mysteriously sacred, containing all of the best and right answers, ideas, and facts that children studying a particular subject at a particular time needed to know. Page after page, day after day.

School is an institution that, when at its best, is controlled, orderly, and predictable in order to organize and control the hundreds of students attending classes. Bells ring to hail the beginning of each subject that will be taught, and students are expected to be in their seats on time, ready to pay attention for forty-five-minute segments. Knowledge is static, there is not much time for questions, and conformity is expected and desired. Behaving so as not to interrupt the others in the classroom requires the ability to sit still, do the work, and listen quietly.

I know this is a generalization, and there are many exceptions to this description, yet space requires me to abbreviate.

When a child is shaped by the expectation of such conformity over and over again for many years, this deeply trains the brain pathways in how to live for life. Conformity spawns conformity. Dependence on arbitrary authorities spawns blind acceptance of what is written or taught. (This is why the Internet and social media news are so pernicious for those who have not been taught to question or think.) What we experience as children becomes the model for what we expect and express as adults.

We also usually picture children being age-graded; in other words, learning certain things when they are six or seven or eight years old and passing from one year of classroom expectations to the next. Reading at age five, multiplication tables at nine. Each child must comply with the expected standards and will receive a grade and evaluation on her work in comparison to the rest of the students.

Because of the number of students, it is much more difficult for the teacher to develop a personal mentoring relationship with each one. Consequently, the influence will be more general rather than personalized.

Sometimes, conformity to cultural expectations and written standards is the measure by which we evaluate each student's progress. If a student creates too much noise, has too many individual demands, or requires too much attention, we have a special classroom for him or some discipline to help him learn to better conform to the norm. Standardized testing focuses on outcome-based answers and does not encourage individuality, initiative, or creativity. Often, this system assesses a child's progress in academics by comparing him to others who are exactly his age and grade.

I understand the need for an excellent base of knowledge, and it does require a plan to achieve covering basics in education. Yet we know that development differs with every child. Some children crawl at seven months. Some do not walk until seventeen months. Some speak in paragraphs at eighteen months, while others do not use many words until they are three and then end up being at genius level as adults. As a mother of four children, I can attest to their differing developmental clocks in almost every area of their lives.

The same happens with learning stages. Parents become fearful when their children do not fit the average and become anxious when comparing their children with others. Actually, there are very few children who fit the "average" mold in every category, including thinking, emotions, physical strength and coordination, creativity, musical ability, vocabulary, test taking, verbal acuity, etc. Often labels are applied to children when they do not perform at an expected age level, when many times they merely need more time to grow into their capacity, depending on personality, drive, gender, and other factors.

As I evaluated these issues, I realized I wanted to create a more personalized model of education. Making the decision to teach our children at home meant we had agency and freedom to figure out how to cultivate an environment where wonder, imagination, creativity, and individual personalities could be expressed while simultaneously providing great resources and foundations for stimulating academic excellence.

Overdependence on Other Authorities

Because of the development of public and private schooling as a historical progression, parents began to shift the responsibility of being the primary instructors of their children from themselves to "trained" teachers and in doing so lost the imagination for being the mentors of their children's lives. Contemporary messages proliferate in the world of parenting:

"Let the professionals teach your children. They can do a better job."

"The system isn't perfect, but children are resilient. They'll be okay."

"I will engage my children when they are old enough to carry on an intelligent conversation."

"My children and I would be at each other's throats. I could never stay home with them or be their teacher."

And yet, from the moment children are born, we *are* shaping deep brain patterns for the ways and values of life. If children are spoken to and read to at an early age, their intellectual ability will thrive and grow. If children are touched, kissed, and embraced, they are much more likely to become strong, healthy, and confident. There is no neutral time of child development. The foundational influence of what is valued, practiced, perceived, given emotionally, and understood at home before the age of four stays with a person for life.

We cannot leave the role of shaping our children to institutions or authorities who do not have ultimate responsibility for their lives. Nor can we suppose that the life messages passed on by those institutions or authorities are in agreement with our own philosophies. Messages are not neutral. They have power and influence. Whether we want the role of teacher or not, it is ours. We do hold the incredible power of parental influence, for good or bad. Even passivity passes on a value to children that says being disengaged is acceptable, though the child experiences a deficit in their longing for relationship.

He Who Walks with the Wise

Do not conform to the pattern of this world, but be transformed by the renewing of your mind. Then you will be able to test and approve what God's will is—his good, pleasing and perfect will.

Romans 12:2 NIV

In regard to education, what does it mean to "not conform to the pattern of this world"? If the world of education is to conform to one way, one right answer, to not question or have significant time invested in wonder, how do we move from conformity to renewing our minds? Perhaps we need to think of a whole different way to enlarge our children's education to be more productive, more fruitful. Questioning and researching the ways children learn best is a productive activity.

What an auspicious thought, that children are inclined toward becoming like those responsible for them. Traditionally, they are learning values by the ways they are taught to fit in, to conform through schedule, peer pressure, and teacher expectations. A mentoring model would move them beyond these expectations of cultural norms. We, the parents, become the guides in their lives to embody integrity, humane behavior, and virtue. Children imitate what they understand, see, and experience every day. How we live is how they will perceive life and act in their own lives.

Every moment, every day, children are ingesting what they see and hear as truth, rightly or wrongly. Parents can pass on what is important to them, accepting the responsibility of becoming the primary model for their children. Learning takes place by what is caught *and* by what is taught, a dual process. Both instruction and modeling are necessary to shape the values of children.

The first years of a child's life are for building foundations of deep, unspoken virtues and the shaping of principles and standards of behavior that will establish a groundwork for what he learns to depend on as truth for the rest of his life.

What Are You Modeling and Teaching by the Way You Live?

If, as Jesus says, the student will become like his teacher, then to become a good teacher, we must examine our own lives. What have I stored inside my heart, mind, and soul? Does my character reflect the integrity I hope my child will imitate? Am I exhibiting the attitudes that I want my child to exhibit? Do I love those around me unconditionally so that my child can understand the love of God?

As I look back over the years, I understand better that when I took responsibility for the shaping of my children's lives, it caused me to grow more into the person I wanted to be. The accountability of knowing I was being studied by my own children helped me to strain toward moral excellence and mature love, modeling what I hoped my children would copy.

> *The accountability of knowing I was being studied by my own children helped me to strain toward moral excellence and mature love, modeling what I hoped my children would copy.*

The growth process for the teacher as well as the student is gradual. Maturity comes over time for both. We do not have to be perfect or feel we have failed if we stumble along the way or make some mistakes. But most important is that we are growing in the direction of our ideals and beliefs and in what we hope to pass on. It takes years for a baby to grow into an adult, and so we have years to access our own potential and to strain toward maturity with grace as parents.

Everything we do—how we work, play, and relate to people; how we speak about politics, worship in church, treat others in public places, and use our phones; what we watch on television and in media; how we treat our neighbors; what we eat; how we take care of our physical bodies; how we use the place of home for comfort, beauty, and love—all of these concepts and more are the substance of what our children will learn. As they breathe in the oxygen of our lives, they will adopt what they perceive is true about life from our behavior and actions.

Adopting New Goals as a Mentor, Teacher, Parent

The teacher or mentor is the first and most profound determiner of how a child will grow in the love of learning and creative freedom to explore and question life and discover answers. The teacher wields great influence and power over what children will learn and embrace for themselves. Below, I offer some specific ideas that were infused in my own understanding of what to pass on.

- If a teacher stands in awe of the physical universe and shows a sense of wonder at a sunset, the delicacy of a butterfly, the variety of color, sound, and design—in all that has been created—then the child will learn to value this. The world around him becomes a place of constant delight, a mystery for pondering, entering into the corridors of his own imagination, filling the file systems of his mind with ideas and classifications.

- If the parent is curious and always learning and brings the child into their curiosity by searching out answers together and sharing what they are learning, the child will also feel free to question, imagine, and share what he is thinking. The student will be like his master and learn the value of research and gain great worth from being able to participate in adding to the research himself.

- If the parent or teacher is comfortable with variety and encourages individuality of personality, preferences, background, and desires, the child will naturally accept the individuality of those immediately around him. In other words, if no student is valued above another because of test scores or an extroverted personality that engages more verbally in life, then the introvert will also feel accepted and will learn to communicate according to his ability, and vice versa—the extrovert will not feel condemned for talking too much. If the teacher avoids comparison and validates differences, then children will become more accepting of one another.

- If a parent gives value to diversity and shows tolerance, the child will, when young, follow the parent's pattern. If the parent is living a life of consistency and authenticity, and the teenager finds that what she has been taught and what she has seen modeled has integrity, she will probably follow much of this pattern the rest of her life. If the parent sees people in their context and exercises understanding and compassion, the child will also have an open heart to the variety of people who come into her life.

- If the parent desires her child to be morally strong, virtuous in behavior, then she must exhibit integrity in life, actions, words, and choices of behavior. Seeing the parent work diligently in tasks, paying bills, organizing life, practicing being trustworthy, the child will learn to love virtue. The parent must make the most excellent goals for how to help the child grow strong in character, in righteousness, goodness, and truth, because the child will learn it in the moments of life spent with her mentor. The child will breathe this reality of life as what she will do and copy.

- If the parent wants their child to honor, to learn to be considerate and polite to others, and value all human beings, then the parent must show honor, respect, and value to their child and to all other people who come their way. When a parent is polite, it becomes the standard for the atmosphere of their "classroom." A child learns respect and manners by the way they are honored, valued, and respected.

- If a parent wants his child to be a person of deep faith and to learn to revere and love God, then he must be consistent in growing in faith, and modeling what it looks like to accept God's love and grace and to give that kind of love and grace to his child and others. Honor begets honor.

- If a parent wants her child to grow in self-discipline and to learn to work diligently, then she must exhibit responsibility and hard work.

- If a parent wants his child to become emotionally mature, then he must practice emotional maturity and learn to generously exhibit affection, ask for forgiveness, and learn to show love.

And so on. Whatever we want our children to learn must be embodied in how we live, what we say, how we grow in character, and how we exhibit our faith. A mentor has the student's long-term development in mind.

Of course, this list is not a guaranteed formula. In other words, we must understand that children have agency and a *will* of their own. They must choose to believe and embrace what is being taught and modeled. But they are much more likely to embrace for themselves what is being taught if it comes with integrity, authenticity, reasonableness, and grace from the life of the teacher in front of them.

Practical Principles for Mentors

A mentor is someone who desires to keep the spark of imagination alive in each child, instead of killing it with criticism or comparison or ridicule.

A mentor desires to draw out the strengths and gifts of the one he is seeking to influence and uses words and actions to affirm and validate the uniqueness of each child.

A mentor speaks forward into the life of a child and desires to draw out the best from inside to help him become fruitful, and to show wisdom in how to go forward. A mentor is also someone who passes on the skills of living wisely.

A good mentor is a symbol of all that is good and strong so that the child is not just taking in factual knowledge, but observing the application of that knowledge in real life.

The parent or mentor will exhibit messages and actions that determine how a child sees her world, how she feels about the whole area of learning, creating, and growing in knowledge, wisdom, and skill. Therefore, the teacher must embody all he wants the child to become.

A mentor is one who is always learning and excited about growing in knowledge, understanding, and wisdom as a way of life.

Picturing my children's hearts as treasure chests where they could gather stories, ideas, ideals, habits, appetites, truth, and knowledge to draw from the rest of their lives, I sought to fill the space in their hearts with all that was good, beautiful, and true.

Yet, I had to possess the wisdom they needed before I could pass on this wisdom. I realized that my intentionality to call them to their best selves meant that I had to be living into my best self. This accountability to who they would become stretched my own muscle and helped me to grow every day as I pursued the ideals we shared together.

Even now, as a mother of four adult children and the spouses of my children, I find that my children look to me to maintain a life of integrity, faithfulness to ideals, and faith and constancy in living out those ideals. In a world of compromise, we, as teachers, can call our students to stay faithful and true in their own character as we continue to embody what we verbally teach.

Indeed, the student will become like his teacher. Committing to this stewardship to become like my teacher, Jesus, meant that I had accountability to grow and become like Him, whom I was following. Becoming mentor and teacher to my children gave me a reason to strain daily toward becoming my own best self.

Wonder gives us a lens
through which we better view
the miraculous, the sacred,
the intricacy of our world
around us and helps form
our spiritual imagination.

4

Mentoring with Love and Lifegiving Influence

Give the children love, more love and still more love—
and the common sense will come by itself.

Astrid Lindgren, author of *Pippi Longstocking*

Greater love has no one than this, that one lay down
his life for his friends.

John 15:13

Jericho is a small suburb of Oxford, England, that borders a canal filled with houseboats alongside walking and biking paths. I was living there when I began writing this book. Most of the homes in this area are connected by shared walls and were built approximately 150 to 180 years ago. Consequently, though the quaint cottages have been refurbished along the way, they are still old and creaky and sometimes have faulty facilities. Mostly, in our little home, the heat was quite inefficient and sometimes imaginary on cold, damp days.

One frigid winter early morning found me cuddled up in my duvet and dreading getting out of bed and the cold, bleak, and creaky house awaiting my presence. At that moment, my bedroom door opened, and Joy, my daughter, peeked in and smiled to see that I was awake. She padded to my bedside and sat down gently beside me.

"Mama, I was thinking this morning. I am just so grateful for you. *I love who you are, I love that we have such great conversations, I love that we get to be roommates this year. I love it that we are such close friends.* I have lit candles downstairs, put on music, and poured you a cup of hot tea so that you can ease into your day."

She gave me an affectionate, heartfelt hug, kissed my cheek, and then padded away.

I mentally took a photo of the moment, because it was so unexpected, but so deeply heartfelt, and it did mean a lot to me. I had not even known how much I needed her words, or her expressed love, as I was feeling a little lost and overwhelmed by issues of my own life.

Though the circumstances of my cold house had not changed, I felt deeply warmed and soul alive. Now I was willing to get up and even anticipated going downstairs to a momentary reverie in which I could ease into the day.

Love given welcomes us into a new day.

Most touching to me was to see my grown daughter choosing to give up time in her busy day to think of me, to serve me, to anticipate my needs.

Our attempts to catalyze our children's imaginations apply also to how they see themselves in relationship to others and to their world. It encompasses helping them to imagine themselves as light-givers and lovers of others. What we sow, our children will indeed reap.

The reward of our taking time to invest the thousands of minutes of love, training, and focused attention in our children is to see them become full-fledged adults. They will have dimension, emotional strength, love that is given generously to others because it has been a part of their experience. To know that somehow they were listening and paying attention as children and now live by the same values as adults is affirming and a fulfillment of what we were attempting to do. Much of our lives we had to take that on faith!

Contrary to popular belief in some circles, love and respect open a child's willingness to learn much more than harsh, adversarial, authoritarian control. Consequently, a mentor must realize that in order to garner the trust and following of a student or child, the child must feel that the teacher is for them and has deep affection and goodwill toward them.

Love: The Secret Power to Influence Our Children

Those anxious to get to the "meat" of homeschooling may wonder why I am placing these chapters first. It is because we have seen many a child who had an opportunity to be well educated by fine academics give up their faith and disparage their family because their relationship with their teacher or parent was performance based or legalistic in nature. *Love given generously has to be the foundation for inspiring our children's hearts and captivating their imaginations with all goodness.*

Awaking wonder in any person happens best in a safe environment, one where there is an expectation of friendship, where love is the oxygen breathed between parent and child, teacher and student. Love inspires one to reach their full potential. Love helps fulfill destiny by inspiring confidence. Love influences learning. Love helps learning to become possible.

The reason I included this chapter is that people asked me what our secrets were for influencing our children. *This is the secret: loving them well, generously, all the time, in every situation.* Giving them a confidence to expect unconditional love from us was, I believe, one of the reasons they listened to us and adopted our own values and faith. *Unconditional love won the day.* This was the power behind the influence we had on their lives.

Why is this important? Because this generous love predisposes our children to want to listen to and follow the messages we teach them and want to pass on.

Love: The Foundation for Positive Influence

Mentors, parents, and teachers need to have a vision for the importance of their role, as mentioned in the last chapter. Also essential is an understanding that acceptance, affirmation, encouragement, and principles of love are the gasoline that fuels the engine of their students' response. Generous, unconditional, accepting love paves the way for great influence and inspiration.

> *Awaking wonder in any person happens best in a safe environment, one where there is an expectation of friendship, where love is the oxygen breathed between parent and child, teacher and student.*

Love exercised, words of encouragement and affirmation, respect given, appreciation verbalized are fuel to human hearts and minds. Love is the air that we breathe in to support the rest of life's demands. Love provides an invisible support system that gives mysterious strength and health to live well in the day-to-day demands.

Being loved specifically and intentionally adds to our physical well-being, our spiritual equilibrium, our emotional health, but also our mental strength and health. The action of love we express is remembered in the heart and mind of a child, offering them scope to exercise giving love as their own practice. When we teach and model this kind of love to them, we are empowering them to have strong relationships the rest of their lives.

Joy's words that day moved me beyond my dread to a feeling that the day was a good one. Not only that, but when I was deeply loved and noticed and appreciated, her action enlarged my heart's response to my world.

Our goal as teachers is not just to reach the minds and imaginations of our children with many facts and ideas. Love speaks forward into their souls and gives vision to nurture inside of them the belief that they have great capacity, unmeasured worth, and abilities and potential to fully become a person of value and importance in their world.

Unconditional love, affirmation, and hearty acceptance are prerequisites for reaching our children's *hearts* with our messages. Love and affection open a child's willingness to listen and pay attention to the knowledge and values we hope to pass on. This is profoundly important in the relationship between the teacher or parent and the student or child. Children naturally want to please those who have taken the time to invest in their lives with personal care for them. Without the engagement of our children's hearts, our instruction is shallow and passing.

Grace and Unconditional Acceptance

Many voices swim in the ocean of our minds, each proclaiming the best way to train and educate children. Often, we live under the illusion that we must have an adversarial, authoritarian attitude toward them, seeking to control their actions and behavior. This philosophy advocates that we exercise that authority and power to rule over them by exuding *forceful* control. They will not respect us unless we appear to be stronger and more powerful than they are. If we love our children too much, we will spoil them, we are told.

Probably the most important influence of my whole life in learning to interact in a healthy way with all people, including children, came from pondering Jesus and the way He embodied lifegiving influence.

Jesus, the Divine Mentor, the Servant Leader

When God entered the world of mankind in human form, He desired not just to save humans from their brokenness, but to show human beings how to live abundantly, how to flourish. The real Jesus was the Christianity that I had longed for as a college student.

As I pondered His life through His stories, His teachings, and His actions, I realized that in order to secure the hearts, minds, visions, and values of His disciples, Jesus chose to give totally of himself, to lay down His life. It required His time—His daily, absolute presence. It required His intentionality, because He knew what vision He wanted to impart to His followers. It required His modeling a life of integrity, compassion, and humility; Jesus taught for three years the heart of His messages, laying aside His position in heaven and sacrificially giving up His freedom, His whole self, for the benefit of His followers. Ultimately, it even required His death so that He could redeem them.

The Cost of Love: Servant Leadership

When I became a believer, my whole life was transformed by studying and learning from the life of Christ as recorded in the Bible. His model of love, humility, and coming as one who serves was exactly opposite from what I had learned in the world.

Jesus' method to reach the world with His ways and truth was to live with, teach, train, and send out His disciples into the world to bring His light and redemption. This pattern was also taught in the Old Testament, as I mentioned in the last chapter, and then embodied in the living Christ.

Christ's life became the model for teaching my very own disciples, my children. His disciples were never perfect, but were flawed human beings, and yet all had been transformed by His messages to such an extent that they were willing to die for His kingdom. I did not look for perfect behavior in my own children but for heartfelt responses, growth, a movement in the direction of maturity and strength. Patience and a belief that serving them mattered kept me going forward.

Christ's way of influencing and leading His disciples gave me a concrete way to influence my children. I think this is often left out in educational models, the laying down of one's life to serve. Love served as a constant stream of messages through Jesus' stories.

Multiple verses capture my imagination to understand what this might mean for me as a mother and as a teacher. Here are a few:

Greater love has no one than this, that one lay down his life for his friends.

John 15:13

This was the basis for understanding the necessity of laying down my life for my children as their parent and teacher.

Take My yoke upon you and learn from Me, for I am *gentle* and *humble* in heart, and you will find rest for your souls.

Matthew 11:29, emphasis added

I understood that to be like Him in living this out meant that I needed to be gentle (kindhearted, soft in response, patient!) and humble—not lording my role in authority over my children, but coming to them with the humility of Christ. I was to bring rest, peace, life into their environment as a purveyor of Jesus.

In everything, therefore, treat people the same way you want them to treat you, for this is the Law and the Prophets.

Matthew 7:12

Jesus taught that the Law and the Prophets were composed by this idea, that we are to treat others the way we want to be treated. In other words, if I wanted my children to learn to respect others, I needed to model respect and honor in relationship to them. If I wanted them to learn to show compassion, I needed to show compassion to them. And so forth.

> But Jesus called them to Himself and said, "You know that the rulers of the Gentiles lord it over them, and their great men exercise authority over them. It is not this way among you, but whoever wishes to become great among you shall be your servant, and whoever wishes to be first among you shall be your slave; just as the Son of Man did not come to be served, but to serve, and to give His life a ransom for many."
>
> Matthew 20:25–28

As a mother, I realized that if I was going to model Jesus to my children, I would need to develop a grid that said, "I am to be a servant leader to my children. As I follow Him, I understand it will cost me my life. I am to give myself as He so generously gave himself." And that this, following His ways, was a part of my own serving and worship of Him.

Teaching my children was not ultimately to please them or to deserve their affirmation. It was out of worship to Christ, to serve Him and emulate Him.

Teaching my children was not ultimately to please them or to deserve their affirmation. It was out of worship to Christ, to serve Him and emulate Him.

Teaching children is a very long-term journey, and it is fraught with difficulties and self-doubt along the way. I was often confronted in my heart with the deep selfishness and lack of patience and maturity I had brought into parenting. But the attitude with which we come to our children will affect much of their response to us as teachers.

How challenging this was for me to learn to carry out little by little. Constantly in my life, I run up against my own selfish nature. The hard work of commitment was not familiar to me. Often I would fail or be impatient or sometimes wish I could run away. Yet my vision for the pattern Christ laid for me kept me going forward, one step at a time. This gave me a way to practice living. And though I made many mistakes, I think learning to love and serve in this way as my children's teacher is probably what won their hearts. This was also the pathway for me to grow into a mature and constant sort of love. Shaping children shapes those who mentor them.

The Costs of Love and Laying Down One's Life

As I look back on many years as a mother, a mentor of others, an educator, the giving generously of my life and putting aside my expectations was exceedingly important to having the impact that I was able to achieve. It is a grid or lens through which to see my life: "I am the teacher, the servant leader, the parent. Even Jesus laid down (put aside, gave up, sacrificed) His life, so if I am to reach my children, who are my disciples, as He reached His, there will have to be a giving up of my own expectations, rights, and freedom to serve them."

I am not speaking of making children an idol. As a matter of fact, the love of Jesus motivated His own disciples to give up their lives unto death, to learn obedience, to give sacrificially. Even as my husband and I modeled respect, we required the same from our children. (More on this in chapter 8, on character.) Yet people often ask me why our children still love God. I think that to a great extent, it was as we followed the model of Christ that we saw His influence over the hearts of our children.

Here are some of the practical costs of serving and showing love.

Time

A secular model of education says, "Just cover the material well—the facts, the ideas, the books, and that is all that is required of you."

Yet because we wanted our messages to go heart deep, it required that we first did what we could to secure our children's hearts by giving them our time, our attention; looking into their eyes instead of accepting a passive response; taking the necessary steps to build and secure a deep and trusting relationship with them. Giving them back scratches, listening to them, staying up way beyond our point of exhaustion, appreciating them, blessing them before bed, praying with them for their needs and heart issues, and serving them were practical ways we extended love in action. Helping them to ask for forgiveness, to make peace when there was an offense, was a regular part of each day.

A Secular World Steals Time and Forgets the Value of Personal Relationships

Secularism has invaded so much of our lives that sometimes we do not even recognize its power to diminish the strength of a life truly dedicated to Christ. When shopping, acquiring, entertaining, experiencing, being pacified, taking care of possessions, and engaging in a constant flow of activities takes the bulk of our time and energy, *we have little left to give*.

This means that there is no time for a natural life—work, productivity, being still, creative play, talking without interruption to become deep friends and to speak of ideas, dreams, desires, compassion, insecurities, doubts. We only have a window of time with our children, and we do not get do-overs. Materialism, the easy acquisition of consumer goods, entraps so many parts of our lives. We do not realize how much things—experiences, entertainment, movies, the Internet, phones, television, cars—take up our time and thus occupy the desires of our heart.

Imagination plays a foundational part even in this aspect of life. When we ponder and wonder what creates health, goodness, character, emotional well-being, peace of mind and soul, we are better able to plan a life around what are priorities for us.

We must be convinced that creating a natural home environment that provides time for relationships to grow is better than having all of the toys to entertain. The conviction that we are using our time well when we invest in personal relationship has to be pondered, imagined, believed. It is only as we learn to embrace this ideal that living out the other ideals will be possible.

Often, I found myself bored, impatient, and exhausted in carrying out my ideals. Though I always loved my children, sometimes I did not like them. Sometimes we must realize that we act because we think something is wise or was modeled by Christ, not because we feel like it. I acted out of my goals, not my feelings, when I was tempted to drown in the details of life. (Just admitting my own immaturity.) Yet, when I kept moving forward in the direction of "real"—real relationships, real creativity, real play and pretend, real companionship and community—I began to see the fruit of this in the lives of our children. I had to learn, over and over, to give up myself and to be content and at peace about it. This is a choice of the will, not feelings. We became a close community, enjoying one another's company, engaging in the same stories read aloud, love building threads that tied our hearts together and to the One we all followed together.

We might find it easier to give our children a toy or gaming device to entertain them than to sit on the floor and play and interact with them—a machine or object to interact with instead of a human being to enjoy and respond to. I learned that I didn't have to "feel" like I wanted to play, I just needed to do it.

What has created this out-of-balance world? Women have confusing feelings and then feel guilty because their lives are lonely and they are isolated from other adults. Women were never supposed to enact this role alone, and feeling guilty for being stressed is not emotionally healthy. Grandparents, cousins, siblings, and beloved neighbors in a close community were the support that mamas used to have. It has only been in modern times, when people do not know their neighbors or attend church with them or have relatives close by, that parents have become so isolated and alone, bearing so much stress by themselves. And we have become used to this way of living so that we do not even recognize why we sometimes feel so stressed, isolated, and alone.

We can all see that humans are not thriving, in general. Despair, depression, loneliness, isolation, and rising suicide rates are common plights. But we must see that unless we return to a more humane and personal way of investing our lives, people will continue to grow more troubled, more impersonal, more distant. (This subject deserves another book.)

When we want to entertain children with cartoons, movies, or online activities so that they will not make a mess with the paints, play dough, bubbles, blocks, or puzzles (or so they won't require hands-on supervision), then we are also making a decision to limit some parts of their minds from being activated and developed.

Secular values are also very tempting to our children because they call to them in every room where they live, in every part of life through available cell phones, televisions, computers, and gaming devices. There is very little space where a child or adult is free from the influence of this Internet world, which calls to them every moment of every day. And it calls to us primarily through messages on our phones and computers.

We must choose to fill the time with planned personal time that satisfies to the depths of their hearts, minds, and souls.

To create a life where the hours and moments can be filled in satisfying interaction means that we must *choose* to fill the time with planned personal time that satisfies to the depths of their hearts, minds, and souls.

If we are going to say no to secularism, with its pull and messages that destroy our and our children's souls, we have to replace it with activity that allows positive, enjoyable ways to be occupied. And that means giving up our time and freedom (as Jesus did), and learning to be creative in using time.

Toddlers, Teens, and Everyone Else Are Wired to Learn by Wondering

To keep a little toddler occupied, we must give our time to read, walk, play, pretend, rock and nurse, hold, sing to, talk to. In a contemporary culture, it is tempting to give in to cartoons or phones or any machine that baby-sits for us. (It is also tempting to think we are wasting our college degree or talents, because life with little children can be tedious when we are always caring for our children alone.) Yet we must resist the temptation of the video baby-sitter, because multiple studies have confirmed that exposing young children to visual media can negatively impact brain development.[1]

Bubble baths, bubbles, shape sorters, stuffed animals, safe outdoor play, walks in nature, etc. must be organized as daily rhythms to occupy babies. God made it so, as He created babies to need us. Throughout history, all babies at all times have been born needing attention and care. It is not unusual for a baby to be dependent—it is a part of God's design for them and for us as parents.

Our family did not live without technology but used it in a limited way—not often, especially in the young years. I would not have lived through the ear infections and all-night asthma attacks without the comfort of the *Winnie the Pooh* or *Little Bear* cartoons. And of course occasional movies helped us through sick days, overwhelming days, and "twenty days of snow" months. And of course, sometimes I needed a movie break, a grace to get through a challenging day.

Each of us must decide for ourselves what is acceptable for our family, depending on season, demands, etc. But the overriding principle is that *devices are never a substitute for real relationships*. Wisdom, not legalism, must be applied and understood.

And so it is with all ages. Children must have time organized around developing skills (pretending, exploring, playing, taking music lessons, drawing, gardening), time to play creatively, chores, quiet times to read and write and create as a way of life instead of being entertained at all moments by artificial diversions.

Teens need to have places to cultivate community, real work opportunities, and ways to serve others. Home can be a great place for that. We hosted movie nights, parties, group meetings, volunteer work, times of serving others, training day camps, travel, etc. to keep our teens busy and involved in meaningful activities involving lots of people with whom they could interact. (*The Lifegiving Home*, which Sarah and I wrote together, has hundreds of ideas.) This kept them from being bored and dependent on engagement with a phone, a computer, or a television. Of course we had these in our lives, but only on a limited basis. Did it take lots of my personal time and effort to engage our kids in outside activities? Of course it did. But I counted the cost in light of what investment in creating social, instructional, and skill-oriented times would produce.

Time is merely a beginning to creating channels of love to children.

Words of Affirmation, Encouragement, and Inspiration

Words have an active power to shape deep pathways in our brains. Words of life and love can create a pattern that will carry messages to children the rest of their lives. Positive words prepare people to feel they have value, that they are acceptable and worthwhile.

"I love who you are. You make me smile every day."

"You are such a great friend and have been such an encouragement to the boys in your art class."

"God must love me a lot to give me the gift of you as my daughter."

"I love your music. It makes me happy to hear you play your guitar."

"Your Lego castle is amazing. Tell me about it."

"I so appreciate your help. You always carry my big loads."

We are shaped by the words that plant themselves inside our memory. One of the most soul-building tools is to intentionally build our children up with words that speak forward in their lives, those communications that will put pathways of hope, affirmation, and value in their memory.

Participating in Life Together

One of the most lasting contributions you can give to children is providing a place where relationships can grow easily and with an atmosphere that is conducive for one to thrive. But as with everything else, to imagine a place and to build it out requires time, effort, and planning, over and over again. Home can be a place where people can belong and become.

All of us need a place where our roots can grow deep and where we are a part of a like-minded community and have a safe refuge from the storms of life. Home can also give wings to dreams, nurturing possibilities of who we might become. But there must be a space to walk in these paths of imagining opportunities and time to unearth the wonderment of what might be possible in life. It was a profound realization when I understood that I could become an artist of life, painting within the walls of my home by shaping a sacred place to share life, to grow deep in relationships, to daily exercise faith together, to celebrate common beautiful moments. (More about this in chapter 10, on a wonder-filled home.)

By my shaping goals toward mentoring my children, our home took shape as a laboratory of life in which our ideals could be discussed and practiced every day, together. All homes will have a personality of their own, but part of loving well is planning the life and shaping the character that will define the unique attributes of the family who dwells there. Legacy is shaped in the walls and in the moments of the days, in ways the loving mentor chooses to carry out ideals in a real-time life.

Legacy is shaped in the walls and in the moments of the days, in ways the loving mentor chooses to carry out ideals in a real-time life.

Since all our children have become published authors, we asked ourselves why this would be. Yet as we look back, we can see how naturally this came to them. Ours was a verbal culture. Clay and I were both people of words, though both of us are introverts. We used words by reading to our children, having meals every day where we discussed ideas, books, philosophy, world view, Scripture. Our asking our children for their opinions on what we were writing, creating, or speaking about was expected by them, and they eagerly gave them. It took so much time to live a lifetime of engaging them in our own work, but writing and speaking became a natural fruit of their lives because we regularly planted so many seeds of a verbal life. Jesus was called *the Word*, meaning "the Message." A message-driven life and a relationally rich, communicative life shapes a healthy trajectory of growth.

Each family culture will have its own unique attributes. Perhaps you are a gardener or farmer, a nurse or doctor, a writer or pastor. Taking your children with you into the worlds that interest you will help them to learn about what you love and will bind them to you with the feeling that they share in your life.

And so it is with other aspects of life. Cooking, organizing, cleaning, gardening, building, music, art, hospitality, ministry are caught by children when taught and practiced as a common occurrence together, in relationship.

The same goes with playing or just taking our children with us wherever we go as Jesus did His disciples. Passing on values, truth, vision, and morals happens over big and small moments, as we are walking through life. Deuteronomy reminds us of the necessity to keep a 24/7 mindset in shaping the hearts of our children.

Physical Affection

A tiny bundle named Lilian entered my life a couple of years ago. She was my first grandchild. Soothing her before she fell asleep was a sweet habit we shared. Holding her tight, I would put my cheek against hers, my mouth near her ear, and I would rock back and forth as I made up Lily songs.

"Mama, tickle my soft back" was a common request in our home. Sarah coined the phrase when she was just beyond toddlerhood. Basically, it was a soft back scratch that had its own name in our home.

Touching children, rubbing their head, kissing them on the cheek, scratching their back, hugging them with a bear hug, massaging their hands or feet with lotion when they're in need of comfort creates actual pleasurable feelings between the one touching and the one being touched. Touch is healing and actually causes those who are ill to have more ability to overcome disease.

Touching a child says, "I like you," "You have worth to me," "I value you."

When a parent makes it a habit to be affectionate to a child in a way that accompanies their personality needs, there is an automatic connection. A shy introvert or teen may be reticent to touch but would feel affirmed by a gentle tousle of the hair. An extrovert might enjoy a strong hug or a back rub. All of us have differing desires. Yet affection is a sure sign of closeness and preference that often softens the instruction of a parent to a child.

Be *for* Your Child

A favorite verse of my mother's when I was a little girl was, "If God is *for* us, who can be against us?" (Romans 8:31 NIV, emphasis added).

To be for someone means that you are their advocate and you will support them, believe in their dreams, and want the best for them. There are endless ways to show love and to provide a foundational championing of our children. The essence of this kind of love is actually a comprehensive understanding of all the areas of love: *"I am for you." "I am your advocate." "I will believe forward into the good things I can imagine for your life." "You can count on me." "I will choose to believe the best about you and help you grow and find support your whole life."*

Being "for" someone does not mean that they will always exhibit the kind of behavior or character we deem admirable. But it is looking at our children with unconditional love and cultivating eyes that see the possibilities in the midst of the "terrible twos" of toddlers or the hormonal teen years.

Now that my children are all full-fledged adults with their own life demands, I find I still play the role of encourager, being *for* them in a world that challenges their faith, morality, and ideals. We become the voice of God's Spirit as we encourage them and help them continue to find that embracing ideals is worth the cost. We are companions of the grace of God.

As we evaluate how to love our children and students well, we must ask ourselves, "Do they believe and feel I have their best interests in mind, or do they think I have my own agenda for them?" "Do they understand that even though they struggle, I am here to help them succeed?" "Is their heart open to my instruction, or is there a wedge of resistance that I need to figure out and address?"

In the end, laying down our lives to love those we seek to influence will open the pathways of their hearts and minds to growth, development, and mental and spiritual strength. The most intelligent instructor in the world becomes a noisy gong or clanging cymbal to the mind of a child if there is not love present in the relationship. But the ones who purposefully and intentionally lay down their lives to do the hard work of loving and winning hearts will find a pathway to influencing their children for a lifetime.

5

Forming Faith through Imagination and Wonder

The greatest legacy one can pass on to one's children and grandchildren is not money or other material things accumulated in one's life, but rather a legacy of character and faith.

Attributed to Billy Graham

I pray that the eyes of your heart may be enlightened, so that you will know what is the hope of His calling, what are the riches of the glory of His inheritance in the saints.

Ephesians 1:18

Dear Mama,

You know the trials and struggles I have been facing the past months. They have felt like a heavy load and going forward one day at a time has been all that I can manage.

But I was praying the other day, and remembered how many times you read us the story of Elijah when he was tired to the bone. And an angel came to him, touched him (a sign of needed physical affection), and then the angel fed him and he slept. I looked up the passage and realized how familiar it was to me because you read it so often. You must have known that someday, I would be discouraged and would need to know that God cared.

Then, verse after verse started flooding my mind, verses that I knew so well from childhood. They spoke to me, encouraged me. I realize how profoundly these verses are still speaking to me today. Thanks, Mama, for pushing through day after day to fill our brain with His love, truth, and goodness. All of those times still live in my brain and heart today and are speaking to me.

Love,
An anonymous Clarkson child

My adult children have all walked a journey of challenges, difficulties, temptations, and times of discouragement since they left home. Their lives have also been filled with times of happiness, adventure, and fruitfulness. Yet, in a broken world, I knew they would need to have the Bread of Life stored inside their hearts to draw from as adults.

The reason I include this and the next chapter about spiritual formation and foundations is because this was a primary focus for opening our children's hearts to the beauty of God. We had a desire to have as a grid for everything we taught a biblical world view, and we pondered how to lay this foundation first.

Faith Formation Is about Reaching the Heart, Not Behaviorism

> I pray that the eyes of your heart may be enlightened, so that you will know what is the hope of His calling, what are the riches of the glory of His inheritance in the saints.
>
> Ephesians 1:18

The apostle Paul wrote of wonder and imagination playing a part in the lives of those who would know Christ. When he prays that the "eyes of your heart" be enlightened, he is saying he desires the eyes of the place inside us—where we have our heart, mind, soul, personality moving in unity to create our inner self—to be awakened to the countless resources of truth, comfort, companionship, eternal love, and sublime beauty of God.

Isn't this what faith is, the seeing with the eyes of our heart what we cannot see with our physical eyes? Seeing with the eyes of our heart combines our mind that acquires truth, our heart that imagines and fills in context and story details, and our soul instructed by the Holy Spirit to understand nuances of light, goodness, and beauty. And so, as we seek to educate our children about our transcendent, infinite God, we show them His reality by exploring what we can all see and wonder at and imagine when we view the art of His night sky. We ponder profound thoughts by reading the Word that tells us His stories and learning about the heavens and creation with our mind, which can study and access scientific details about stars and galaxies and synthesize it together. But to fully engage in the transcendence of God, we must imagine, wonder, and ponder the truths, His creation, and His story.

The Power of Wonder in Imagining the Story of Faith

God created us to soar, to dance, to fly—to live with gusto as we enjoy and discover the magnificence of the mysteries He has strewn throughout creation. He longs for us to hear His whispers throughout the day, to see the shadows of His ways moment by moment. Not only that, but He also promises to walk with us through each day. Just as the sails catch the wind, letting the boat glide effortlessly through the water, so when our hearts are filled with the Spirit of God, we move ahead through life unburdened and with more ease. Faith in God must be passed on in every generation as a foundation of how to live, how to see life, how to serve God, if our culture is going to keep Christianity alive. And the fragrance we leave with children must be something beautiful and authentic.

> *Faith in God must be passed on in every generation as a foundation of how to live, how to see life, how to serve God. . . . And the fragrance we leave with children must be something beautiful and authentic.*

Longing to spark imagination about this reality meant bringing the literature of the Bible to life. Approaching the stories of the Bible expands all of our understanding of the in-the-flesh person of the God who created the world, Christ. We ponder how He lived, what He was like, what He valued. Again, using our imagination, we wonder just what He was like in a world that was real and teeming with people of differing cultures, personalities, convictions, and character—or lack of it.

As we teach the stories of Scripture, we set the stage by imagining the scene together. Through pondering, we conceptualize what it was like to walk the dusty roads packed with adults and children, dogs, cats; to hear the Roman guards riding on horses, spears in their hands, yelling and pushing people out of the way; to hear the sounds of lambs bleating on the way to market; to understand the thirst and sweat and smells surrounding Jesus as He walked the roads of Jerusalem and shopped at the markets. Wonder gives context to the words Jesus spoke. We imagine with our children, "There was a little boy just like you who loved to run and chase his dog." Or, "Maybe in the fields, a girl just like you collected a bouquet of wild flowers as she heard the comforting words of Jesus giving the Sermon on the Mount." Without imagining what the atmosphere was like, who the people were in the story, what their needs, fears, and demands were, we do not get the whole context. Entering into the story as a real-time experience opens our hearts to the messages given there.

As we imagine, we make alive the reality of those thousands in the crowd, old and young—a white-haired woman hobbling with a crutch, a baby in arms crying desperately for the milk of her mother's breast; people by themselves or in families; some poor in tattered clothing, the wealthy Pharisees in long robes with tassels; people with various health issues, the blind, leprous, crippled; those oppressed by the taxes and legalism of their day who were "like sheep without a shepherd" (Matthew 9:36).

Then we better understand the balm of Christ addressing them with the comfort of His words, "Blessed are the poor in spirit" (Matthew 5:3). We have not just heard words, but we have seen these precious, exhausted, confused, overrun, discouraged people in the pictures of our minds' making. We experience the miracle of a God who is infinite coming as a man to give comfort to the oppressed. Jesus is not just an abstract god, giving moralistic rules to follow. He becomes a compassionate, humble young Jewish man, submerged in the complex pool of humanity and bringing love, truth, and virtue to life. His reality moves us to see with compassion those in our lives who live in the roadways of our day. This is what I wanted my children to ponder—a real, living God who had feelings and relationships, who brought light, truth, and beauty into the reality of frail humanity. Our hope is to nurture an authentic faith.

We must open the living stories of Christ and the Bible to our children in a way that makes them tangible. It is as we imagine, ponder, engage that we are able to ignite the imaginations of their hearts. We ask, "How do you imagine this story setting as you ponder the people around Christ?" We seek to get at the *heart* of God to engage the heart of our children. Then we pose more questions: "What are the crowds of people like that we pass and see every day in our worlds? What are their needs?"

Living Authentic Faith through Our Days

Most would agree that we are living in challenging times. The media speak every day of disasters, political doom ahead, and wars and devastation all over the world.

How important it is, then, that the education of children includes the spiritual formation of their hearts and minds so that we may empower them to cultivate a faith that will last through all the difficult seasons. Opening the imagination of their hearts to "see" the reality of a God who loves them, who cares, who builds their character that they might be strong, who is willing to love them wherever they are every day, who shapes the way they will look at their lives every day.

When a child has seen the galaxies in their grandeur, when we give the creator of these stars a name by telling them His real-life stories, they put a name to the designer of the universe as well as the humble carpenter who redeemed them. Then, we teach the concepts and embody His words in our own flesh as they learn His words and watch us model these words every day: "Love one another";[1] forgive "seventy times seven";[2] "learn from Me, for I am gentle and humble in heart."[3]

When we enflesh our love and worship of Him through the real, daily moments of our own life, our children's imagination of what they are seeing, hearing, and living becomes for them a reality. Faith is an authentic response to what they have imagined through creation, stories, and reality. Coming to believe in this God, their heavenly Father, their protective shepherd, appeals to the yearning of their own heart. Then faith, with the eyes of their heart, is a natural response of their own childlike belief.

Consequently, a life of wonder and imagination also plays a foundational part in the area of faith. When I sit with a child wrapped in my arms and watch the sun come up and say, "Just look at the sky that God painted for our pleasure this morning," a child imagines God as the sublime artist of all that is interesting and good. God is the creator of sparkling sunshine, of purples, yellows, and oranges. The child has someone to thank from a heart full of pleasure in enjoying the beauty given.

We twirl and dance to rhythmic music and laugh and sing and say, "Just think, God made us to hear, feel, enjoy, and sway to music that goes deep into our being." We smack our lips as we feast together on bubbling creamy potato soup with warm bread and melting butter, affirming, "Aren't we glad God thought up butter and chocolate and all the tasty things we get to eat every day?" As we do these things, our children learn that God is dimensional, the One of whom it is said, "O taste and see that the Lord is good" (Psalm 34:8).

When we lead children to observe the intricate beauty and coldness of a snowflake, the warm morning sunrise in summer, the softness of puppy fur, the flash of lightning, the boom of thunder shaking the skies, the sound of music that causes them to dance, the beauty of swans gliding across a lake, the taste of strawberries, or the crunch of pomegranate seeds, they experience deep satisfaction in the world around them. Then we thank God often for the beauty, the artistic design of each leaf, the color of each artifact, and we say, "If you imagined your own world, what would you have created? Doesn't our artist God have the most amazing imagination?"

It requires time to notice, to dive deeply into the waters of artistic design, playful imagination. Consider peacocks squawking, ducks waddling, snakes slithering, and children become even more aware of the design and diversity of their world and the broad pleasure their playful God had when He imagined what He would place in their world.

When they perceive the creativity of the artist Christ and learn to thank Him for a moment of beauty or pleasure, He becomes personal, intimate in their thoughts and experiences. God is more than a philosophy to be known, more than a theology to be espoused. He is a mystery to ponder; a loving Father who created so much beauty and pleasure; a holy, sacred Creator to worship; a Savior who showed compassion; a mysterious wind blowing through their lives to cherish.

Knowing that their God took children into His arms to bless them as their parents cuddle and bless them causes their imagination to understand that God is a personal God who wants us to be comforted in His arms.

We verbally value in their presence the hidden person inside themselves, who can think, love, dream, create. We speak to them of their beautiful personality, the gift of their own story to tell, the place they have in God's greater story, and of using exactly who they are to show His light, His love, His intelligence, His holiness, His humility, His compassion to their world.

Children's imaginations are fueled from infancy to wonder about their Creator, to imagine Him in relationship to them, to grasp their agency to create, love, and influence their world as He did. Understanding that He made them to be like Him gives them a sense of purpose, dignity, and meaning that satisfies their heart's longings, even at an early age, even if in immature but growing understanding.

Bringing God's Light into Our Darkness

At times it feels that every moment is a battle. Perhaps it seems too idealistic to imagine diving into life every day seeking to embody the beauty, freedom, love, transcendence of God when there are dishes to wash and messes to sort out. Yet it is possible that we need to ponder and remember that God wants us to live fully, wholeheartedly in the love, grace, and mystery of "God with us" every moment, every day. Inviting Him into our moments, worshipping Him as we work, is a part of our own faith walk. Bringing light into the darkness is a part of our real-life expression of faith.

Likewise, our children will hear of wars, tragic car accidents, devastating storms that kill hundreds, illnesses that consume the lives of loved ones, and darkness that accompanies life in a broken world. Tragedy and death will touch each of our own lives. When we walk alongside our children through their questions, when we seek answers in Scripture together and talk of the kingdom yet to come, where all tears will be dried, all hearts comforted, and all wrongs righted, they will begin to store up in their minds and hearts the truth of "In this world you will have trouble. But take heart! I have overcome the world" (John 16:33 NIV). They learn courage and joy by listening to your messages and watching you exhibit, by faith, the courage and joy you speak of. You are a living picture of faith.

Preparing our children to understand the darkness, the battle for truth and beauty, and their opportunity to become warriors for Christ's cause is as important to their long-term stability as it is for them to know first that He is the source of all goodness and light. It would not be realistic to show our children only the beauty, because to understand the need for His sacrifice, they must eventually, when they are old enough to understand, ponder death, evil, and the brokenness that comes from being separated from Him. Young children need protection from the evil of the world. Yet, as they grow more mature, their questions about life and death will arise naturally. You will know when to begin sharing about the complex issues of life. Not too soon, but as they grow and begin to question, that is the time.

Children are deeply insightful, full of intelligence and good questions. Longing to have a life that has purpose, each hopes to become a hero in her own story. Paving the imagination of our children to understand they can be light-bearers in a dark world gives them a sense of stewardship to bring hope in and through the stories of their lives. We build vision by imagining together how to become people who bring light. We honor every bit of their pondering and all of their doubts, listening to their insights so we can encourage them to dig deep. Then the foundation of their faith can better stand against all onslaughts of culture and voices that challenge their beliefs. They will be familiar with the battle because they have journeyed through it in their imagination of stories heard and life lived.

> *Paving the imagination of our children to understand they can be light-bearers in a dark world gives them a sense of stewardship to bring hope in and through the stories of their lives.*

Spiritual Formation Developed through Practical Goals

Practices of wonder shaping were planned into the schedule and rhythms of our days. Setting specific goals and placing them into a real-time schedule means the shaping is more likely to happen systematically over time.

Daily devotions

A teacher cannot pass on what she herself does not have. So of course the beginning point of helping to shape a strong faith in the lives of children is to be growing fresh in our own faith.

Surprising to me was that all of my children have memories of getting up each morning and finding me pajama-clad with my hot tea and a little candle lit, diligently reading my Bible and often praying. It was a habit from college days. Sometimes these times with the Lord involved my own pouring out of fear, anxiety, questions. Other times my heart was dry or exhausted. Sometimes I was filled with joy and worship, others times just plodding along.

But even as a great home estate is built one brick at a time, so my legacy of investing in reading, studying, and loving God's Word came one day at a time, one brick a day to build a bigger legacy of faith.

If we are people of faith, then understanding and expressing that every day out of our love for God must become a heartfelt commitment. We each have only one life to live to tell a story about Him, about His ways, about His love. And if we are Christ followers, then God calls us to use our gifts, to exercise our faith, and to become salt and light right where we are, especially as parents.

So, because I needed to swim in this reality before I lived it out every day in real time, I committed to this spiritual discipline. This habit alone shaped my children's lives and habits deeply because it was "what the Clarksons did," every day, all the time. I will write more broadly of this in the next chapter.

Exposure to the Word of God, the Bible

Research suggests that babies are abundantly open to the world they are born into and that they learn, perceive, and form values from the first days of their lives. Then, slowly, in the early years of their childhood, it is theorized, many of the parts of their brain are closing because they are already formed by the things they have learned and understood as they were immersed in their world of wonder.

How important it is, then, that children hear the stories of truth at young ages. We read dramatically (Old Testament and New), memorized some of the wisdom (Psalms, Proverbs, the words of Jesus, admonitions of the New Testament), and learned the history and responses and stories of faithful as well as rebellious people throughout (Genesis—the beginnings; the Pentateuch, first five books of the Bible—the boundaries God set through law, admonition of parents to pass on His words, His desire to bless the Israelites and the consequences of rebellion and choices against His wisdom; the stories of good and bad kings—this really grabbed my children's imaginations because they learned that choices had consequences by seeing these consequences in the lives of real people; Psalms—songs filled with praise, wisdom, prayer, and laments of real people).

The exposure to His wisdom and truth is not forced, but is the oxygen that is breathed as a natural rhythm of life. Memorization of passages together meant that we would all hear the voice of God speaking to us the rest of our lives, as the Bible is God's vocabulary. Memorization, a little at a time, becomes a sort of game and challenge. "Do you think we can say all five verses today? Let's see."

We memorized a number of these together, such as Psalm 1, the first verses of Psalm 19, parts of Psalm 37, many proverbs, Joshua 1:8–9, Matthew 6:33, Philippians 2:1–11, and more; Proverbs should be read aloud several times throughout life, and at least once through a child's years at home. Isaiah was a favorite prophet, and we memorized some passages from Isaiah and Jeremiah. Then, of course, the gospel accounts of Jesus must be read through all the years. And finally the letters of the New Testament, with passages to memorize. (Reference *Educating the WholeHearted Child* by Clay and Sally Clarkson for more on this topic.)

Numerous children's Bibles are great to use with little ones. But giving each child their own Bible at the age we thought appropriate helped them to see themselves as a part of worshipping God.

Discipleship as a Way of Life

Education is discipleship. Whoever inspires learning is not passive but is actively passing on a world view, whatever that world view might be. How important it is, then, that we seize the opportunity and freedom to help our children see the world through eyes of faith, with the values we esteem foundational. Observing the life of Christ became my model. He walked through the normal days of His disciples, loving them, teaching them, serving them food, showing compassion for their exhaustion, healing their relatives, answering their questions.

And so, living with my in-house disciples gave me an opportunity to seize moments of teachability to pass on an essential understanding of truth as we observed Jesus together. It is not the goal of the teacher to merely pass on head knowledge, moralism, or legalism, but to pass on a real, lifegiving faith that addresses the needs, hopes, desires, longings, feelings, and questions of a person in daily relationship with God.

Head knowledge, learning and understanding wisdom and doctrine, feeds the mind with how to organize life, how to live wisely, what is "righteous living" in the eyes of God. In an age when virtues are not taught or embodied, we must give our children a systematic understanding of what is right, pure, and just.

Though profoundly important, head knowledge must be passed on in relationship to the living, personal God. Dogma and philosophy can become rote, dry, meaningless to the heart unless they are explored in a way that illumines the heart to see and worship God. We teach that God is infinite, omniscient, exceptional, and beyond the confines of our human definition. And then we spend an evening outside observing the galaxies above.

And yet in His humility and steadfast love, He condescended to become human so we could begin to know Him and relate to Him as His friends, His beloved children, as Scripture says. It is relationship with Him we were made for, and Scripture captivates with His incarnation to elucidate His reality. Next, we scratch their backs while singing to them, give a hand massage with vanilla lotion, or help them clean up a mess they have made.

Moral Foundations vs. Moralism Indoctrination

Learning moral biblical foundations shows us how to live and gives confidence about how to make wise decisions in a variety of situations. Biblical principles of morality are gatekeepers and show us how to walk in wisdom. We all need guidelines to help us maneuver through a world filled with foolishness. Children who are taught a foundation of goodness vs. selfishness and rebellion have more security and confidence to know how to live in their world. The Ten Commandments, Proverbs, and the New Testament books are filled with wise instruction.

Yet, children must also understand that no one is capable of acting out true goodness or being perfect at all times, because all of us are flawed and selfish. They learn of God as their heavenly Father who will companion them and lead them on a pathway of maturity and righteousness. They understand Jesus as the one who wanted to redeem them from evil inclinations and sin, and the Holy Spirit as the indwelling God, who will lead them to learn how to live wisely and in God's ways.

Religious dogma without the vibrant enfleshing of the truths learned can give the idea that all one must do to please God is to know the right philosophy and the most important memory verses to be a mature Christian. Legalism without considering the needs and well-being of people who were sheep without a shepherd became the disdain of Christ.

Moralistic legalism, teaching Christianity as a list of rules to keep, can suggest that our relationship with God is based on our works. This misleads one to think Christianity can be limited to the right behavior and the keeping of rules. It also leads to judging others we perceive to be not as "good" as ourselves and a separation of the religious from the rest of the world.

Moralism focuses mostly on the rules of conduct. Be good, and don't sin by doing these bad acts: murder, stealing, adultery. This method overemphasizes law versus living and tends to minimize the character, the heart, and the engagement required from us to reach out to those who are lost. Motivation for living for His kingdom becomes lost in the rule keeping.

Moralism makes Christianity a black-and-white, reductive belief system. Often, Christians who are moralistic focus primarily on behavior as a way to measure faith. Moralism also separates us from the heart issues. All people will fail, and all must learn to understand God's grace and redemption and daily cleansing of their lives.

Moralism says, "If I can just get my child through high school without them getting pregnant, on drugs, addicted to pornography, or dependent on the wrong kind of friends, I will have done my job." But this kind of training depends on merely doing what is right and avoiding what is wrong, the performance of works.

Instead of only giving a view of the works of morality, we want to pass on a living vision of why morality is important. For example, instead of saying that immorality is wrong, evil, we paint a beautiful vision of why choosing purity is beautiful. We cultivate in our children a heart that will love the sacredness of honoring marriage, their own body, and the value of another person. We want them to view life with an eye for serving others so that they will have a heart motivation and a biblical imagination about why it is important to be pure, steadfast, strong. We desire that they cultivate and become committed to a vision of marriage as the community God created to give comfort, legacy, faith, accountability in the world, because they have so deeply experienced this kind of love in their own family. Moral virtue stems from heart vision, not just moral instruction.

Legalism is establishing faith based on rules or traditions that measure a mature believer primarily by their actions. Give a tithe, go to church, know all the right things to say, don't sin. It ignores our desperate need to receive God's mercy, grace, and forgiveness because we will never be able to live up to all the rules. It also neglects to teach compassion for others, humility, kingdom living. Since the questions of life are much bigger than rules, our children need to see the Christian life not merely as behavioral, but as an organic relationship with a Person who loves and responds and engages with His people.

Theology: Wondering about the Nature and Reality of God

Instead of emphasizing rule keeping, our focus was on God himself, His nature, His attributes worked out in real stories. Our little ones *need* to be taught what is right and what is wrong by a beginning instruction of what Scripture lays out for us. Then we proceed to deeper theology, the study of God, His history, and His words. Understanding that God is preeminent and beyond human beings' attempts to quantify Him teaches us to worship Him, to stand in awe, to rightly serve Him with our whole hearts. We pass on the mystery of an infinite God that we can know more and more over our whole lifetime but can never limit to our own personal, historical, or cultural biases. Since God is infinite, there will always be more to know about Him.

As children strain toward adulthood, they require greater understanding of more abstract issues such as the cancer of sin, the explosive and cruel nature of a world separated from God, how faith is the bridge that carries us through the times when we do not understand but still choose to believe that God is good. Faith leads us to understand the nuances and mysteries of a real walk with God. Humble appreciation for the grace of Christ in our lives predisposes us to have compassion for those who are separated from His love and redemption. Jesus wants us to raise our children to see the compassion in His heart toward the lost and then to go into our worlds with the same compassion and a desire to reach out.

In other words, we want our children to have hearts that understand why living a righteous life is the best way to live sustainably for them and for others. And we want them to understand the very nature and attributes of God, to move toward their heritage in Christ. We want them to realize that God gave us guidelines to show us how to best live life because He loves us so much and wants us to flourish. A heart for what is right is not just a knowledge of some right things to do, but a growing desire to move in the direction of living a righteous and just life from the heart. When temptation comes, and it will, just having a moral law will not carry them through. But having a heart conviction for why something is meaningful and important will guide them to want to move in the direction of what is true for themselves and all people.

24 Family Ways

Clay, my husband, wrote a devotional for our family that thousands of families all over the world have used, *Our 24 Family Ways*. We desired to give our children a language of spiritual terms, and we wanted them to understand the ways of our hearts that would lead us to understand the heart of God. We came up with 24 Family Ways that would lay a foundation of knowledge, behavior, and heart responses to God so that our children could grow confident in knowing how to develop spiritual muscle for themselves. This also gave us a place for training our children to learn to love and embrace biblical values. (This devotional and the accompanying coloring book are available on Amazon.)

Prayer

Becoming familiar with speaking to God about all issues of life comes from making prayer a daily engagement. Praying at our table before each meal, praying at the end of devotions for all that is on our hearts, praying before bedtime, praying when a child was distraught and needed comfort, and spontaneously thanking God for something beautiful (a shooting star, a newborn baby, a sunset, the aspens shimmering, a hike in the mountains, or an answer to prayer) made talking with God a natural way for all of us to communicate with Him, because it was natural to us, their parents.

Maturity causes us to understand that we are not in control of circumstances, people, or outcomes. We need to have a place to go in our minds and hearts and an idea of how to pray to ask God for His help when we understand we have no other hope than Him. And practicing praying to Him every day helped our children understand that He would be with them always and present to companion them through all of their days.

Church

Experiencing our own challenges through nineteen moves, seven times internationally, made finding a church difficult. This was especially true when our children were in their teen years and everyone began to have an opinion about the service, the youth group, the music, the preaching.

Adding to that the fact that many of us are very idealistic in our approach to life means that often we will not find people who identify with all of the ideals we live out. Yet our involvement in church is an expectation of Scripture; church is where we will meet, hear and embrace the Word of God, find accountability and friendships. Church is the place where we find a community of people who will journey with us through all seasons and is essential to our growth and well-being.

So finding and regularly attending church with others was a foundation upon which we made a commitment as a family. We met with challenges along the way, understanding that Christians are flawed, which is also a part of spiritual formation. Slowly, learning the value of staying, being loyal, growing in a church setting gave an understanding of what faithful commitment looked like. Learning to serve and help others as a way of life, giving generously of our time and skills, gave our family a way of seeing church not just as a spectator activity where we sat back and criticized, but as a place where we participated and sought to please the heart of God. In the end, a couple of our children prefer praise-band, evangelical services. The others prefer more formality with liturgy and readings. But all fellowship together in unity and community of worship of our God, which was our goal.

Active Ministry

A necessary part of spiritual foundation has our children incorporate into their self-image the conviction that faith is not just knowledge, but works itself into a life of serving and loving others, as Jesus did. Serving others in some way as a normal part of life must be practiced for children to develop a self-image of one who has something to give. Serving others catalyzes the knowledge stored up as a way of learning the truths in practical moments of life.

Many have asked Clay and me why our children still have a living faith in God. God's grace and mercy for us is one of the main answers I give. We were not perfect parents and did not live a perfectly virtuous life in front of our children. Yet we did follow our ideals as much as we were able in this messy world.

One of the factors I see that really shaped their sense of self was that we served others as a family. Hosting our own moms' conferences over twenty-three years meant that our children had to set up book tables, decorate stages, work at registration tables, speak, perform music, pray with people who had real needs. They were involved shoulder to shoulder with people, helping them, seeing their needs, learning how to reach out. We considered our children a valuable part of our ministry team. We explained when they were older that their lives were a living book of encouragement to those who were just starting out in shaping their own families' spiritual formation.

Our children participated with us in the evenings when we would meet with other adults before the conferences began. Training for each area of responsibility, being in a community of thirty-five people serving side by side, and praying together left a deep imprint on their lives of what personal ministry done together looks and feels like.

Then for two days we all would work tirelessly to serve hundreds of people at each conference. When it was over we would all go out and celebrate—the kids would go with their friends and have cheeseburgers and fries, which seemed like a splurge to them. Then a swim in the hotel pool topped off the evening. We had staff dinners where we ate, shared in friendship, and sort of fell apart at the end of a long weekend.

I think that this and many other ways we did ministry together helped shape their personal imaginations that they had a stewardship in the world to serve others, to encourage, to mentor. Their faith wasn't just a head or heart knowledge, but led them to reach out, to act on their beliefs by loving and serving others. They each perceive that they have special skills and personalities to bring God's light to their own arenas.

Developing a self-image as servants of Christ to bring His love to others grows over years of living out ministry. There is no one way to pass this on; every family can be creative in reaching out to others. Yet outreach is on the heart of Christ, and to understand His giving of himself to us means we practice together giving ourselves to meet the needs of others, to know more what it means to allow Him to incarnate himself through us.

Mentoring as a Way of Life

In reality, we are the gospel message our children will read. Our acts of kindness and thoughtfulness, our willingness to admit our failures and ask for forgiveness, our delight in and thoughts about God's Word shared through all the moments of life will open our children's hearts to His reality. Through this enactment of faith in the moments of our daily lives, our children will be able to imagine a God who is good because they have seen His goodness expressed to them in their own lives in a million ways by us, who model His reality through our own life of wonder-filled worship and love.

Our children draw our accountability to live a faith-driven life, and yet, because of feeling responsible to live faithfully in front of them, we grow into our own spiritual potential. Serving through our home becomes a laboratory of our own faith and life.

A heart for what is right

is not just a knowledge of

some right things to do,

but a growing desire to move in

the direction of living

a righteous and just life

from the heart.

6

Heartfelt Faith That Never Stops Growing

Just as a nursing mother cares for her children, so we cared for you. Because we loved you so much, we were delighted to share with you not only the gospel of God but our lives as well. . . . You are witnesses, and so is God, of how holy, righteous and blameless we were among you who believed. For you know that we dealt with each of you as a father deals with his own children, encouraging, comforting and urging you to live lives worthy of God, who calls you into his kingdom and glory.

1 Thessalonians 2:7–8, 10–12 NIV

As the deer pants for streams of water, so my soul pants for you, my God.

Psalm 42:1 NIV

Nurture: To care for and encourage and facilitate the growth of something or someone.

My lanky teen was spread out full length on our den couch, eyebrows furrowed, looking pensively up at the ceiling as though studying something there, hugging a squishy, old, much-used pillow to his chest.

The day before, he had come to my bedroom and whispered so that I could barely hear, "I need to talk to you about something. Can we find time when no one else is around?"

The next afternoon, Clay was off to do errands, and I asked him to take the rest of our clan.

A cup of hot chocolate and fresh cookies graced the table between my son and me, as I hoped a sweet bribe might help open his heart.

"Mama, have you ever felt something inside that feels kind of like hunger, that you long for something you can't quite define, that you have deep desires for something beyond this life? Mama, is that what it's like to want to know God? To make sense of life? To find His love? I think some of what you have been teaching me my whole life is finally making sense, and I wonder about it a lot."

All of my children had come to me with such questions and feelings, sometimes afraid of the questions that bombarded their minds and filled their hearts with confusion. Many times of doubt, times of disappointment in the behavior of believers, times of failure blew through their minds. But also there were times of amazing insight and inspiration that helped me to keep going, to stay faithful.

Wonder opens inner doorways to endless rooms in the castles of our children's imaginations. Systematically, we pass on a body of truth, stories, wisdom in all the days of our children's lives as a natural part of life. Then, they engage their imagination and wonder about how to synthesize what they have been taught. They have thousands of memories, ideas, and stories to put together. Training, teaching, experiences, and a modeled way of living have been stored inside. Wonder and imagination flow out of what is stored. This becomes the basis, the foundation that informs their agency for making good decisions in life. The Holy Spirit uses all this to prompt thinking that leads to faith and to wise choices.

Looking to a little one, a middle schooler, or a teen with understanding and sympathy helps us to aim our words at their felt and real needs. We must remember what we felt like as teens and understand the angst as our children move from the secure, predictable world of home into the wide, mysterious world beyond. Sometimes our children don't need another lecture about "how not to doubt" or "my apologetics to help you believe."

Often, what all of us need is a friend to tell our deepest thoughts, a massage to relax anxiety, a time of quiet to restore, a friend who walks with us and companions us through our storms and joys of life. And so our children need and long for our friendship.

Much research tells us that young adults are leaving their faith more quickly than any other generation. I hope this chapter will provide more ideas and inspiration about how to reach hearts and spawn self-wonder for your children to imagine a life of faithfulness.

Bringing Lifegiving Moments into Faith

Sometimes adults take themselves too seriously, but often comfort, a back scratch, a hot cup of tea is needed instead of an admonition. Life is serious, of course, and we want to impart all of the truths, ideas, and theology that we can so our children will have a vast reservoir of insight stored up. Yet maturity is a very long process, and insight comes over time; that requires work and rest, as with our bodies. Human beings have a mind, but also a body that needs to eat, rest, and restore; emotions that need loving input and encouragement and pleasure; and a soul filled with desire, ponderings, and dreams that needs to be fed and guided.

We are not in control of the universe or our children or our lives. We cannot, by being anxious or exerting neurotic force, cause our children to grow or to believe. Resting in God's love and providence, we wait in peace and with love to support what is going on inside our children because we choose to believe God is faithful. Acknowledging that passing on faith is a natural process of the way we live with our children, knowing there is no formula for success—only time, love, and faithfulness—leads us forward.

We cannot, by being anxious or exerting neurotic force, cause our children to grow or to believe. Resting in God's love and providence, we wait in peace and with love to support what is going on inside our children because we choose to believe God is faithful.

Once someone asked my daughter Sarah why she thought all of our children ended up with a strong faith of their own. She quickly replied, "I think it was because of the warm French toast covered with salted pecans and drizzled with maple syrup. We enjoyed our lives a lot."

Another time, Joy had experienced the death of a young friend who was ill; she had prayed for him, but he had not survived. The same week there was a shooting at our church. A family member of her friend was injured, and several other people were killed. She was, understandably, deeply troubled at these dark events as a twelve-year-old. I would never have chosen for this to happen to her at such a young age—or ever! She poured out her heart through many tears. I hugged her, listened to her. Then I made fresh cookies, some hot chocolate, and popcorn, and we watched a favorite movie, sitting close together. She didn't need answers, because I didn't have answers to solve the "why" behind the atrocities. But I could offer a safe place of love, rest, and comfort. My children have never doubted that our world is broken, because life did not allow that.

Wonder also plays its part in our lives as parents. We must imagine and wonder about what our children were wired by God to long for and to need. Friendship is at the top. Each of us longs to be loved, to have a significant life, to have a work to do or a story to tell; we long for justice, to be a hero in our own story, to grow in and access knowledge. So as we looked inside our children's longings, we attempted to point them to God for the fulfillment of what they were created for. In other words, we sought to appeal to their longings and desires that were placed there by God, not just give them a moral or directive to follow that was separated from real life. But we also recognized that they were a body, mind, soul, and heart.

Recently, one of our adult children was quite exhausted from work and study and had more of that ahead in the coming months. The next week was a birthday, so a party was held; twelve people attended a feast of my famous (in our family) fried chicken. Then, as is our habit, everyone in the room was asked to share something they loved or appreciated about the birthday person. At the end of the night, I got a call from the adult child, who said, "This evening of celebration was just what I needed. I have been so isolated by mountains of work. So many people said such wonderful things to me. I forgot how much I need my friends and community. I felt so loved and appreciated. I still have the same amount of work ahead, but I am filled up and feel like I'll make it."

Passing on a legacy of faith to a child is an organic, natural, relational process. Passing on the life of Christ is making real His love, beauty, artistry, intelligence, compassion, truth, humility, and heart for His children through the actions and heart of our own lives. Sometimes our action is making a great meal, watching a movie, going on a trip. Or playing games and hosting parties. We celebrate life, shake it up a little, have fun together.

Like a shepherd who leads his sheep to lifegiving water and pasture, our first responsibility as a parent is to lead our children to the lifegiving presence and reality of Christ, considering the needs, preferences, and ages of our own in-house sheep. We must also be creating a sustainable, centered, and pleasurable life for ourselves so that we can be a source of joy, pleasure, comfort, and companionship as well as a teacher.

Have you ever visited a church and caught yourself thinking, *The spirit here seems so lifeless*? There can be organized teaching, even some acceptable music, and yet *something* is missing. The seemingly right things are *done*, and things are done right, but the Spirit of God does not seem to be alive and moving in that place.

The same can be true of many Christian homes. A home can be filled with praiseworthy Christian things and activities and yet still seem lifeless. It just doesn't seem as though the Spirit of Christ is alive there. Good Christian parents can be highly committed to their children and even be very skilled home educators, yet they still may fail to bring the life of God into their home in a way that their children sense His presence, vibrancy, spirit of love, and reality there every day. Our faith must reflect integrity between beliefs and behavior.

That is why we consider nurture to be the first, and perhaps most essential, step to building a biblical Christian home. Although it is not a concept you will hear much about in relation to the more measurable and visible priorities of discipleship and education, we are convinced it is the missing priority in many Christian homes.

As a parent you must lead your children to the lifegiving presence where you are cultivating a multidimensional life of rest, play, work, creativity, learning, and outside engagement in the world. Your desire should be to implant a longing in their spirits for God that can be satisfied only with the Bread of Life in Christ, who "plays in ten thousand places."[1]

But let's remember, the shepherd led the sheep to green meadows of sweet grass, wild flowers blowing in the wind, sunshine or rambling clouds, a bubbling stream of cold water, safety from storms and dangerous predators.

And so we recognize our own flourishing takes place when we also consider passing on messages through pleasurable days that are also filled with chores, meals, and responsibilities.

No matter how good your church may be, a few hours each week cannot create the longing for Christ that God has uniquely designed you to impart to your children. You are to be the primary lifegiving presence of Christ to your children, through His Spirit living and working in your life as a Christian parent. Remember, indoctrination is not the goal. Legalism, basing faith on works that focus on the right laws to keep, the right rules to follow, is also soul killing if that is all that is offered.

We have observed this as all of our children have ventured into a very secular world that holds different values and foundations of truth than we held as a family. Rules and formulas did not hold them fast in their faith.

It was actually the community of belonging that we built, the traditions and fun, the growing knowledge and love, embracing their roles to be light-bearers in their lifetime, and their understanding of a personal God engaged in the real issues of the world that held them fast to the faith of their youth.

The "Christian" world can be filled with hypocrisy, judgment, arbitrary expressions that violate the heart of God. He who came to reach into the dark world with His love and light came as a real, in-the-flesh person. And so if our children have not experienced or been introduced to the living God by breathing in His reality day after day—even in the midst of disappointment with other Christians—and by watching us model the compassion God commands us to have, they will not find that rules and indoctrination will hold them. Children who grow up in a home that is alive with the Spirit of God and whose spirits are nurtured and fed are more likely to become life-living and lifegiving adults. It's all about nurture.

How Do We Nurture?

When Paul was teaching the Thessalonians how to pass on a legacy of faith, he used the image of a mother who feeds and cares for her children. He also used the image of a father who "deals with his own children, encouraging, comforting and urging you to live lives worthy of God, who calls you into his kingdom and glory" (2 Thessalonians 1:11–12 NIV). His image of discipleship was like that of a mother and father tenderly caring for, encouraging, feeding, and nurturing the faith of their children.

Each letter in the word gifts stood for one of the five areas I held as a grid in my mind to focus on each day: grace, inspiration, faith, training, service.

We held a mental model of how to view discipleship moments in the life of our family every day. We pictured each child's heart as a sort of treasure chest, as I mentioned in chapter 3, filling it with truth, memories, serving, loving and receiving love, stories of

Christ, and all that we found to be good, acceptable, and true about Him. We wanted them to be filled with the knowledge and reality of God, but we also had a desire for them to live out of full hearts to bring His love and reality to their own worlds. Faith is never to be held in a receptacle, closed and kept inside, but as a living treasure chest from which to draw in order to send treasures of His love and reality into the world.

I needed a practical plan for each day to know and understand what I wanted to impart in these discipleship moments. We came up with a model that worked for our family called Life Gifts. Each letter in the word *gifts* stood for one of the five areas I held as a grid in my mind to focus on each day: grace, inspiration, faith, training, service.

Our model focused on three priorities within each of these areas of nurture.

Training or discipline is the process of influencing your children's actions and attitudes. Your goal as a trainer is to build godly character and habits in your children (see Proverbs 22:6).

Instruction or teaching is imparting Bible truth to your children. Through instruction, you are helping your children grow in understanding, wisdom, discernment, and faith (see Ephesians 6:4).

Modeling is being a living example of your training and instruction. You are showing your children what Christian maturity looks like and encouraging them to imitate your example (see Luke 6:40).

Grace

The gift of grace is the desire and ability to relate personally and purposefully to God and people.

> Jesus replied: "'Love the Lord your God with all your heart and with all your soul and with all your mind.' This is the first and greatest commandment. And the second is like it: 'Love your neighbor as yourself.'"
>
> Matthew 22:37–39 NIV

The gift of grace is what I want my children to receive from God, to know that He loves them unconditionally and will always love them. Then out of the grace they have accepted and received, I want them to learn to extend that same kind of unconditional love, grace, and acceptance to those who come into their lives.

Every day I still am looking for moments to model, teach, and train my adult children to live into God's grace and to guide them to extend God's grace to their siblings, their parents, their friends—to practice giving the gift of grace.

Inspiration

The gift of inspiration is the desire and ability to view all of life in the light of God's sovereignty and purpose.

> For we are His workmanship, created in Christ Jesus for good works, which God prepared beforehand so that we would walk in them.
>
> Ephesians 2:10

All people long to know that their lives and their actions have meaning and purpose. I want to inspire my children to understand that God created them with their personality, their skills, to do good works in the world that will bring God's light and truth to bear in a dark world.

I seek to read them inspiring stories, to give them heroes who lived faithfully. We speak forward in their lives of what they might do to bring light, to spread love in their stories.

Faith

The gift of faith is the desire and ability to study God's Word and apply its truths to every area of life.

So then, just as you received Christ Jesus as Lord, continue to live your lives in him, rooted and built up in him, strengthened in the faith as you were taught, and overflowing with thankfulness.

Colossians 2:6–7 NIV

Faith has two heartbeats. The inward beat is the taking in of Scripture: reading it, memorizing it, talking about it, and pondering what it means.

Then, in light of what we understand of God's ways, values, stories, admonitions, wisdom, I want them to learn to apply that faith in the outward beat, in the actions they practice in their world, understanding the truth of God's Word, and then living out serving God by His input.

Training

The gift of training is the desire and ability to grow in Christian maturity in the power of the Holy Spirit.

Train a child in the way he should go, and when he is old he will not turn from it.

Proverbs 22:6 NET

Training involves laying a foundation of godly character in the heart of a child. When the child's imagination is captivated by seeing himself growing strong inside, by being able to learn what it means to be diligent, faithful, telling the truth, living by wisdom, then we want to offer practice in developing godly character. (More on this in chapter 8, on character.)

Service

The gift of service is the desire and ability to minister God's grace and truth to the needs of others.

Do nothing out of selfish ambition or vain conceit. Rather, in humility value others above yourselves, not looking only to your own interests but each of you to the interests of the others.

Philippians 2:3–4 NIV

Service gives our children a sense that they, like Christ, were called to be servant leaders in their own world. Practicing serving others throughout childhood gives them a familiarity with reaching out to others as a way of life and helps them recognize needs. Again, what we practice, we become. Involving our children in serving by our sides in our own twenty-five years of conferences prepared each of them to own the idea that they were also called to give, love, serve, and reach out. Giving our children an understanding that all believers are called to take light into the world by giving them real ways to serve as children set the course for their adult lives.

Why Purpose Matters

"I wonder how God is going to use you to bring His love into the world? You are such a great friend; I think many people will feel the love of God through you."

Many educators leave the important aspect of purpose out of their children's education, and I think that neglecting to engage their whole faith training in actively living out purpose is why many fall away from their faith. They have not connected knowledge to their own story, their own vision of what they were made to do.

Because our children left home feeling a sense of purpose, this meaningful call on their lives helped them to stay faithful to the biblical ideals we held as a family. They could see a reason *why* they should be faithful because they knew that their lives and their choices had an effect on others. The accountability to the vision they had for life kept them seeking to live by the vision for ministry we had all cultivated together. The idea that we each had a part in the race of life, and that we were passing the baton to them to carry on a legacy of faith to their generation, captured their imagination.

We hoped that we could pass on a way of seeing their lives that would allow our children to understand that they were created for the purpose of taking God's kingdom message into the stories of their own lives and into the relationships they would develop. We also wanted them to see that they were capable of bringing God's truth, life, light, and beauty into their personal world—that they were the ones who would carry a legacy of faith to their generation.

Teaching, training, and modeling to our children how to serve others actually gives them a sense of self-worth—that they have something to give to their world, some way to serve so that others might be helped. Our home was a spiritual laboratory of life. Besides working at conferences, working at the homeless shelter, teaching a children's class, taking meals to those who were ill, hosting hundreds over the years in our home, our children developed a sense of self. The voice of their imagination said, *I can serve; I know how to encourage. I am able to help. I can teach and train others. I see people's needs, and I think I am the one who is supposed to reach out to help.*

As we look to the life of Christ, we see that He walked alongside His disciples and befriended them. Daily, He instructed them in the ways of God. They served beside Him. His sending them out to learn and practice ministering to others gave them a sense of confidence about how to meet others' needs, so then it was natural for them to go out into the world, as Jesus commanded them, because they had learned, had watched Him, and had a pattern for how to live this reality for themselves by pondering the life of Christ.

Living on purpose gives a reason to be faithful.

Living on purpose gives a reason to be faithful. Having our children walking alongside us as we model helping others gives them an understanding that they also are called to reach out to others. Many young adults in our culture today don't understand the connection between their faith knowledge and doctrine and their purpose in life.

Some Messages to Teach

Arming our children with an understanding of what ideals, commitments, messages are on the heart of God guided them to know how to make decisions in their own lives based on their knowledge of these truths. I will offer just a few of the life messages we shared. But you can come up with your own list. It is necessary to teach and discuss contemporary issues that our children will face in order to arm them with the knowledge of how to battle the philosophy the world may offer in disagreement with their heritage of faith.

In light of the cultural battleground for capturing the imagination of young adults, we wanted to prepare our children to know how to *think* about and make life decisions from very orthodox, biblical values.

The Ten Commandments, Loving God, Loving Others

God provided a short, concise list of directives that give good boundaries to help us live safe, sustainable, righteous lives. The pillars of these messages are essential to loving and serving God. Of course, the first commandment leads us to the whole focus of our Christian life:

> You shall have no other gods before Me.
>
> Exodus 20:3

The starting point for our whole faith is that we were made for God. We find our life in God; He is our salvation, our truth, our wisdom, our love, our Creator, our everything. Christianity is not about religion, church, good behavior, but about us submitting our whole lives to God. We also taught the words of Jesus when we taught the first commandment.

Jesus said there were two commandments that summed up all the Law and the Prophets:

> He said to him, "'You shall love the Lord your God with all your heart, and with all your soul, and with all your mind.' This is the great and foremost

commandment. The second is like it, 'You shall love your neighbor as yourself.'"

Matthew 22:36–39

Combining these two commands and "no gods before Me," we asked engaging questions: "What could that mean? What are other gods in our culture? Can they actually meet our needs, love us, give us wisdom, help us?" We pondered this along with "What does it mean to love God with *all* of your heart—affections, passions, dreams, loves? Soul—your art, music, faith, values, recreation, things you value? Mind—thoughts, ideals, philosophy, what you read?"

We wanted our children to understand that just as we had a relationship with them based on love, pleasure, honor, trust, the Christian life was about cultivating that with God. A lifelong covenant relationship of love, loyalty, honor, worship.

Loving Others as Ourselves

The second part of Jesus' summing up of the Law was about giving our lives to love others, all people, always. Memorizing many verses on loving well and pondering how Jesus exhibited love as the centerpiece of His life predisposed our children to see their life in terms of giving it away for the sake of others. Giving a legacy of loving others pushes against natural selfishness.

Honor

Honor was a very important message on my heart that I wanted to pass on.

We taught our children to honor us as their parents by helping them learn to submit to our requests with respect, no eye-rolling, no sassy words, no refusal. Of course unfolding honor as a family value took lots of time, training, talking, disciplining.

When they learned to honor us, they were practicing being able to bow their knee before God as adults to honor Him. We are the visual example of what it looks like to serve God with humility. Giving value, worth, respect to God is the basis of our humility and worship, and the willingness to serve Him with our whole hearts came from practicing it in real relationships in our home. The obedience prepared their hearts.

We modeled honor, instructed them in honoring others as fellow creations of Christ, walked with them in honoring others, and we spoke of its glory through the days of our instruction. We also had to correct them when they did not honor. Using the 24 Ways and studying Bible passages helped fill their imagination of why it was important.

The Sacredness of Marriage and Family

Giving our children vocabulary and value for the family helped them to have a vision for why marriage would be profoundly important to them as adults. Providing words for and assigning value to marriage and the roles of men and women is also profoundly important for our children living in this confusing secular world today. God created marriage to provide companionship and community to help us live together in all the seasons of life with all of its demands. It was the first institution through which He established an ordered community. Partnering in life with a like-minded, same-faith, and same-purpose person means that you get to build a legacy, a story together that will become a heritage to pass down to the next generation. It is a sacred covenant, a picture of God's always faithful commitment to us.

Sex is a gift provided by God in marriage for our pleasure and as a picture of our union. Through physical intimacy comes the blessing of children and the building of family. Having children is a gift and a result of the love you share. Building a family unit, valuing children, means that you will have community, love, stability, and belonging together. As a family, you get to invest love, faith, and help in those who, in a sense, belong to you. Family is a legacy of life to hold all things dear together.

I never knew how much I would love being a family or how deeply satisfying it would be. I loved building our heritage and rituals that held us together. The experience of our belonging to one another gave our children an imagination for what they would want to choose and build in their own lifetime, because it gave them such comfort and companionship of life and ideals. Vision also gave them a reason to be morally pure. But it must be talked about so that the reminder of why sexual purity is important will speak to their brains in times of temptation, which will surely come.

There are so many more messages we undergirded and affirmed over the years. There are also complex messages from the Bible that must be discussed in your home so that your children can hold orthodox views of God's design as they go into the world. Yet, deciding what messages you want to speak into the hearts and imaginations of your children for the rest of their lives is worthy of your own planning and study. There is not enough room in this book to cover all of these important issues.

Deciding what messages you want to speak into the hearts and imaginations of your children for the rest of their lives is worthy of your own planning and study.

Prodigals, those who choose to leave faith behind, will and do come from homes where faith was cherished. Adult children have their own will to make decisions about how they will live. On top of that, the world is a very difficult place in which to live out faith.

Yet, as parents, being intentional to pass on faith is the best way to stir up an imagination of what it means to know and love God and to choose to be faithful in all moments of life. We train, instruct, model because *we* want to love and serve God. Not all children will respond as adults, and some may fall away as the prodigal son did.

The work of evangelism and discipleship, even in our homes, is a work of faithfulness to God, a worship of Him. He sees our heart and honors our faith and faithfulness. Even as He appealed to His own disciples in love, nurture, and service, we find it is the pathway for us to pursue as parents. And this pathway will cause us to grow spiritually and understand the fatherhood of God even more.

7

A Wonder-Filled Mind
That Pursues Treasures
of Knowledge

You may have tangible wealth untold;
Caskets of jewels and coffers of gold.
Richer than I you can never be.
I had a mother who read to me.

Strickland Gillian,
"The Reading Mother" (one of my
mother's favorite quotes)

He who walks with wise men will be wise.

Proverbs 13:20

Large, feathery snowflakes spun round and round, waltzing through the pine forest outside our living-room window. Six inches was expected by nightfall. Celtic music played moodily through the room to match the dark mountain shadows beyond the trees. Always, every day, all the time, there was some kind of music wafting through the rooms. Piled against the bay windows, all four children were mesmerized by the elegance of the huge, soft flakes and captured by the quiet beauty of the snow as it began to pile up on our wooden deck just beyond the window.

Hot cinnamon cider bubbled on the stove as I poured hot popped corn into five bowls to munch when we would hover by the warm stone fireplace to read together. This was not a day to leave the house, but it was a day to celebrate magical moments together.

As I gently fetched the tray of festive mugs of steaming cider, Joel offered to bring the popcorn as we settled in for the morning reading. Most days found us sequestered in this room, sharing and engaging in a rousing book together. Trained by the familiar routine, everyone knew what to expect. I always read first thing in the day, after breakfast and devotions, because there was always a chance I would fall asleep while reading out loud if I waited until the afternoon. Like most mamas, I rarely got enough sleep.

Why not munch on popcorn and sip cider while reading? Not every day was graced with such fare. Other days I gave blank art paper for them to draw what they were listening to and wondering about, Legos to construct cities and cars for imaginary highways, play dough to create with, outlines of art classics to fill in using colored pencils. The rule was that everyone could do something while we read as long as they were able to listen and narrate back to me what was read. I always threatened to read the whole chapter over if they could not narrate. And of course some days were interrupted by "He sat on my side of the couch," or "Her toe keeps touching my foot, and I can't concentrate. Tell her to stop!"

Yet, because this was an expected rhythm over time with understood standards for behavior, most days were predictably reasonable. What the oldest children have learned to accept and model becomes an un-verbalized standard for the younger ones. All four cherished this daily rhythm as one of the favorite memories of their lives and as the habit that shaped their souls. My son Joel has even made a partial profession of dramatic reading by recording books on tape because of his love of reading aloud.

The heart of a reading home brings joy to shared relationships, because we are all being shaped and formed by the imagination of what we are engaging in together. A sort of mutual intelligence and understanding through the discussions we shared and things we wondered about out loud formed patterns of imagination that fueled our children's intellect. Pathways in our brains are forged as we repeat words and ideas over and over again. Intellect is developed as pathways connect from other brain roadways made over time. Exponential connections produce vocabulary and universal understandings of complex ideas, and the mental muscles become stronger with each practice of reading aloud.

But more enthusiasm, more wonder, more excitement energizes listeners if the literature is well written, intelligent, heart- and mind-engaging. And because the corpus of what we are learning is not for a test but for the beauty, integrity, and intelligence of the story itself, there is great room for wonder to journey broadly in the mind.

Having reasonable recreation or fun snacks to heighten our pleasure made our reading times the pinnacle of each day. I truly think that my children thought math and language arts were what encompassed home education, because they did not even realize that the reading was the core of their learning. Somehow, this time was pure pleasure shared amid varied personalities and eruptions of occasional immaturity and restlessness.

> *The heart of a reading home brings joy to shared relationships, because we are all being shaped and formed by the imagination of what we are engaging in together.*

And I must say, I was quite diligent to make our reading happen for thousands of days of our lives together.

Patterns of a Word-Rich, Verbal Environment

Long before this, I had realized that there was a limited amount of time in each day. I was constrained by this boundary and could only cover so much material. And, as I mentioned before, I wanted my children to be exposed to the best artists, finest composers, outstanding writers, stimulating thinkers. I chose books that would engage my own interest as well.

Determining the priority of reading thirty to ninety minutes every morning (depending on the demands of the day) helped me to cover a broad and deep smorgasbord of subjects, ideas, and interests through the years. Purposing to cover the corpus of our reading together meant that all were shaped in the community of like-minded thoughts. There never would have been enough of me or enough time to use "age-graded" textbooks for humanities (literature, history, biography, classical art, classical music, geography, science, and nature), which were the main subjects of our reading.

I also considered this an important part of my mentoring time—to inform and lead them to wonder about great ideas and to encourage thought processes.

If I had attempted to use an age-graded curriculum (texts especially for first grade, second grade, etc.) and focused on textbooks for each child according to their age, I am quite sure I would have been overburdened and frustrated. I never would have been able to cover all of the material. I knew I would be pressed to get through it all with four different ages of children; as a matter of fact, I knew I would never even be able to read through all the textbooks for each age. Wanting to have all of them swimming in the same waters of intellectual thought also meant there was a special connection, belonging, and community of sharing the same knowledge and scholarship.

Understanding that this required a leap of faith meant that I believed forward in the fruitfulness of this philosophy, but had no assurance of what it would produce. Providing a feast of read-aloud material and a diet of great books for individual reading time added to the assets of their minds. Because I desired to stretch their mental muscles on great resources, I had to focus the way we would do this.

Some of what were common in the genres we frequented were age-old classical literature, illuminating thinkers who specialized in their fields, captivating literary stories, the intrigue of world and American history, the principles of leadership and heroes, and science and nature writers we had grown to love.

What I discovered was that entering into rousing tales, great adventures, historical battles, and romantic tales does open children's minds to wonder about infinite ideas, dreams, and creative possibilities and to truly enjoy the beauty of learning and growing.

Defining Our Goals, Establishing a Firm Inner Structure

A variety of educational philosophies can be effective in forming the intellectual habits and preferences of children. Many teachers have perfected their educational influence according to their personality and preference. Charlotte Mason, classical models, whole book, textbook, education with no boundaries, and unschooling proliferate the education world as the best ways to educate. And there are many creative options among the books available in the home education marketplace covering a variety of subjects.

I have seen that these methods all have their merits, and when they are practiced by engaged teachers, students will grow and develop well. Yet no model is perfect and no education allows a child to emerge without some holes in his learning experience. We called our own philosophy Whole Hearted Learning, a way to nurture whole children, healthy in heart, mind, soul, and strength.

With endless books, resources, and a variety of subjects to cover, it is impossible to completely cover every fact and detail of learning. And there is no magical list of subjects that encompasses all of the most important areas. No formula for education will be completed. Learning is for a lifetime. Relax! Finding the perfect education model is a phantom worry that often hovers over the fearful consciences of parents who choose to teach.

If we gave our children great food for thought, so to speak, and gave them an appetite for how satisfying learning could be, they would be able to access anything they wanted to learn for the rest of their lives. Developing the desire to learn was foundational to our children's growing in mental muscle and acquiring more education the rest of their lives as a personal habit and goal.

We also knew that if we neglected their spiritual formation in our education model, we would have failed to pass on what was the most important knowledge of their lifetimes: to know, love, and serve God; to practice hospitality and reaching out to others; and to follow His kingdom purposes the rest of their lives.

Providing great freedom to grow and learn and mature at their own pace was a value for us. Yet we also wanted to direct them, to lay a foundation, shaping their intellects with the best materials we could find.

Understanding that one of our deep desires is to feel that our lives matter and have purpose also drove us.

If you could use X-ray vision to see the skeleton of our education model, it would comprise the bones or body of education. In other words, even as a body needs bones to hold muscles, veins, internal systems together, so there is a foundational structure holding our system of education together. The bones comprised reading, discussing, writing, creating, facilitating wonder, imagination, and engaging in learning. Great literature, biographies, history, theology, science and creation resources, and the Bible were the food our brains consumed.

The Place for Curriculum

Certain subjects required a line-upon-line, specific step-by-step sort of instruction. Teaching our children to read happened from a straightforward book that was simple and effective, one lesson every day or two. Next, understanding the fundamentals of sentence structure and how language works led us to search for the simplest, easy-to-understand, basic language arts resources, which took just minutes every day. These books built upon systematic exposure to language and grammar basics without being overwhelming in their demands.

Conviction that a verbally rich environment is what nurtured the best of creative writers and intellectually equipped adults meant that we did not use textbooks for grammar or for creative writing. Often, curriculum is so comprehensive, sometimes tedious, and broad that to tackle a book of hundreds of pages is unnecessary and overwhelming. Math and simple language arts were primarily the only textbooks we used. We trusted our children to become great writers because of the rich verbal environment we practiced morning, noon, and night. We did have excellent resources in the books we used, and we did require discipline of study through our rhythms and routines. (More on this in chapter 11.)

Math is a concept that holds the whole universe together. Several resources show the mystery of numbers and the miraculous ways the universe was designed with numbers at the base. These books help give the reason for knowing and learning math. Covering at least one math curriculum a year for each child, according to their ability, and at least one series of language arts workbooks each year simplified my academic purchases.

> *Creative, interesting, highly photographic, colorful, and artistic resources for basic reference books about cultures, science, nature, and geography found their way into book baskets all over the house.*

Creative, interesting, highly photographic, colorful, and artistic resources for basic reference books about cultures, science, nature, and geography found their way into book baskets all over the house.

The middle school and teen years were the times when our children branched out by choosing some of the sources they would read, foreign languages, photography classes, graphic and web design courses, and other creative instruction they desired. There are some excellent literature-based curriculums to use as guides to great books in differing subjects, with questions and other resources connected to them.

Instead of using a creative writing curriculum, we engaged our children in writing poetry, essays, catalog copy, stories, and book reviews and in helping us with our own writing. Because all of our children are published authors and gifted communicators who inspire many people through their books, podcasts, articles, movie scripts, and blogs, other parents want to know how we "did" it. Most are asking for a curriculum or a formula.

We did not use writing curriculums. Creating a generous verbal environment, reading thousands of pages of books with excellent vocabulary and rich language, laid the pattern in our children's minds so that sentence formation and vocabulary were already there. Having each child research and write about areas of interest guided some of their writing projects.

Discussing and writing about what they read was how they learned to talk and communicate, much as a child derives their vocabulary from the sentence patterns they are surrounded by. Great communication and message making followed naturally. The books we read together and the ones they read alone each day were what formed them into excellent writers and communicators. There is no curriculum that can make someone into a great writer if they have not filled their brain with great writing. Great literary sources shaped the pattern for their brains.

Like comes from like. So great thoughts and excellent literature produce great thoughts and patterns of expression in like manner. If one aspires to become a great writer or communicator, one must regularly invest in great books and great messages from excellent writers and communicators and then discuss them.

The Process of Shaping a Reading, Verbally Rich Atmosphere

That I could read to everyone even though there were eleven years between the oldest and youngest had become a precious gift that we all shared together. Little Joy, who was six years younger than the next oldest sibling, always got a picture book at the beginning of our time together, and sometimes the kids would take turns reading it to her. This was to be sure she felt a part of what we were doing, and they actually took pride in becoming teachers to her. We set a standard of dramatic reading, enthusiastic voices. And of course, my older ones had their own reading and research lists compiled for afternoon reading on their own.

Looking back, I better understand that even though her speaking vocabulary was not equal to her older siblings', Joy's capacity to understand stories, to integrate ideas, and to engage in a book was present. She had been inadvertently trained to sit still and listen with all of us since she was an infant because she wanted to be included in "the gang."

It was a part of the expectation of her mind, emotions, and thought processes to sit with all of us. She would rather sit and play with a Beanie Baby or color in a book and be with us than to be by herself playing somewhere else. And now I see that all of this ingesting of expanded instruction was what prepared her to graduate from high school at fifteen and from college by the time she was nineteen, complete her master's degree by age twenty-one, and be the first of my children to finish a PhD degree. She and her debate partner also took first place in the nationals at the university level. She says it was because of our endless reading and interesting dinner-table discussions. I learned that we often underestimate capacity when we only attempt what is the normal expectation.

Four Steps for Cultivating a Rich, Fertile Intellect

Planning my reading year was always fun, and each year was different. Units of world or American history were a foundation for each year. Exploring reading lists and books about books, I would choose a couple of picture books on the subject, at least one nonfiction book, and one or two historical fiction books to read aloud. I would read these books three times a week for our reading time. Each of these units of study usually took six weeks to two months.

Next, I would take a few weeks to read a work of literature, a biography or other nonfiction book of my choosing, until it was completed. This way, I covered essential history and literature, our core, systematically. Yet I was also able to read aloud hundreds of fiction books. Because I did not put myself under pressure to do both at once, we were free to enjoy history and geography and world issues and then just enjoy great literature for its own merit. There were four steps that made the most of our reading experiences.

1. Explore, excavate

Before I started a unit of history or a book of fiction, I would always plan, excavating, digging for an understanding of the context of the place in time, culture, and circumstances. These were the places where exploration into the subject and excavating interesting details about the subject or places of the book we were going to read helped the book come to life.

For example, if we were reading *Treasures of the Snow*, one of my favorite pieces of children's fiction, I would have everyone participate in developing an understanding of the background of the book. Patricia St. John was the author, so I would assign someone to do a short report about her life. (She lived through World War II, lost her fiancé to the war, and never got married. She had spent time as a child in Switzerland, where the story takes place, and eventually became a missionary to Morocco. She wrote children's books to help them understand and imagine their relationship to God.)

Because the book takes place in Switzerland, we would find it on the world map and learn its context in Europe. Then I would assign one or two children to do short excavating research about Switzerland. This led to them finding out that Switzerland was neutral in wars and made a political commitment not to take sides. While exploring, they found the folk story of hero William Tell. I found a beautiful, artistic, illuminated book with his story, and we read and enjoyed that together. This led us to listen to the *William Tell Overture*, a piece of classical music written by Rossini. Listening to it throughout the week, we would read a short biography on the composer from our resource book of composers.

Finally, the time period in which St. John wrote this book was directly after World War II. We looked into short articles that described post-war Europe, the devastation, the disheartenment of the people, and the bitterness that was developing as a result.

As we read the book, we found that the themes were about hateful, hurtful circumstances; difficult responses; and the issue of bitterness or forgiveness. I won't give the book away. But St. John found herself swimming in the waters of great disillusionment with loved ones and friends after WWII, and she wanted to write a book to show the destruction that a bitter heart reaps, as well as the healing of a heart willing to forgive.

Reading this book also led us to read *L'Abri* by Edith Schaeffer, also set in Switzerland, where her family established a community and center to help children and families adjust to life and to heal after WWII.

Instead of spoon feeding each child by being the lecturer-teacher, I sought to develop them into treasure seekers, using their own imaginations to research and find interesting facts. There was also value in giving them the opportunity to add to the interest of the subjects, seeing themselves as having something to offer to one another. Sometimes there were no assignments. We just enjoyed reading.

A lifetime of researching the context and background of books we read would fill the treasure chest of my children's minds with facts, data, ideas, philosophy, convictions of all sorts. Then, when they added layer upon layer of knowledge by doing this again and again with countless books, their brains connected the dots and extended pathways of connection to all sorts of knowledge they had explored. And though we did not do an extensive study of geography or details of all the history of each culture, they connected their memories

> *A lifetime of researching the context and background of books we read would fill the treasure chest of my children's minds with facts, data, ideas, philosophy, convictions of all sorts.*

of countries and historical progressions to all of the books and ideas we read over the years. Consequently, their knowledge of countries, ideologies, philosophies, cultures, and politics was great because of their own engagement, research, and exploration of these subjects.

We took one day a week to read about classical artists and observe their paintings; to listen to the music of classical musicians and learn their stories; to read natural or physical science or creation magazines or books, with a bit of geography thrown in.

So Monday, Wednesday, and Thursday, we read aloud either history or literature. Tuesday was art, culture, and science. Friday was field trip day—adventuring to a museum or nature center or concert or movie—a day to have fun outside our home.

2. Engage, immerse, experience

Next, I would actually read the book every reading time, for a half hour to an hour and a half at a time, until we finished it. That would be the core of our morning reading. Of course, many times, especially when reading great books of fiction, classics, the kids would often beg for "just one more chapter."

As an aside, our taste was vast and highly developed. Our souls and mutual appetites for life were shaped by the same stories, same ideas, same moments shared. We feasted on a banquet of books of every kind: all varieties of fiction; historical novels; classic literature; also captivating tales such as *The Lord of the Rings*, THE CHRONICLES OF NARNIA, *Freckles*, *A Girl of the Limberlost*; biographies of leaders, missionaries, inventors; science and nature; an endless list of subjects.

Historical biography was a favorite genre. Science and nature helped us enjoy our world and curiosity about it. Reading biographies of great classical visual artists throughout the ages while observing their famous renderings inspired appreciation of eras of art. Classical musicians and their stories accompanied by their rousing music also captured my children's imaginations.

We covered political thought (when they were older), lots of theology, philosophy, humorous stories that caused everyone to roll with laughter.

Often subjects moved us to the practical: architecture, landscaping, cooking, photography, the art of diplomacy, and the keys to winning friends and influencing people.

Yet this is what I call the engagement or immersion stage where we spent hours just reading together through thousands upon thousands of pages of a variety of stories, books, and ideas.

3. Express, discuss, expand ideas

Next was probably the most profoundly shaping habit of our lives as a family. I attempted to capture this process in my book *The Lifegiving Table*. I believe our family is part hobbit. We loved to eat, we loved to feast and talk, celebrating merry moments together, wiling the night away in sharing opinions, ideas, humor, conviction, and friendly community.

Our meals were often simple. "Someone heat up a box of organic tomato soup." "Would one of you kids slice some of my homemade bread and cheese and make some grilled cheese to munch with the soup tonight?"

Candles would be lit, music would always be wafting in the background (only instrumental would do for a background to conversation), and then the important part of all of these readings would take place.

"Tell Daddy about what we read today." "What did you like about Patricia St. John's story?" "What do you think it would have been like to live in England after World War II with cities and homes destroyed, marriages destroyed by so many deaths, heritages lost?" "What did you like about the story of William Tell?" "Shall we play the overture while we are sitting here?"

Exercising wonder and imagination while personally engaging in the thoughts and ideas of a book by expressing them, defending them, mulling them over is as useful to the brain as lifting weights is for building muscle. Lifting intellectual weight and pushing it through the corridors of our thoughts shapes mental strength. Each person traveled pathways of their own imagination, and shared thoughts spurred on more individual and communal thoughts.

Developing a culture of a love of words and a value for expressing opinions also helped each of our children develop life convictions, a commitment to virtue and character, and an understanding of the value of morality lived out in a real life and of the meaningfulness of hard work and self-sacrifice. Our dinner table was playful, with games of intellectual imagining and romping through countless millions of ideas.

And honestly, this practice cultivated each of us into becoming best friends with each other. Because we shared so many endless hours swimming in the same ideas, reading the same books, discussing the same messages where every opinion and engagement was valued, in the process of eating together day after day and making it a time of shared heart and soul community, the strength of our mutual values and commitments became a part of what defined us as a family.

It takes time to carve out an ideal. When there are a lot of littles, dinner-table discussions may only happen once in a while and may be about what Little Bear said to his papa. Don't try to force things too early that you want your children and husband to eventually love. All in good time.

Please do not assume that this was always an orderly process. Arguing broke out from time to time, and immature and selfish attitudes sometimes surfaced. Disagreement and hurt feelings had to be dealt with (training manners!). Personalities clashed. And yet the commitment to shaping a loving and generous soul community by this habit was one of our most profoundly influential practices. It gave a broad and strong foundation to our children's intellectual development. So manners and relationship skills were built in the swirl of more than sixty thousand meals shared together! (That's just a little bit over three hundred a year, so it could have been much more in eighteen years.) So use these thousands of times strategically.

4. Evaluate, review, play

Each child, through imagination and wonder, took in what their personality and mind dictated. They synthesized material from books according to their own capacity and interest. At the end of a book, we did not have to do book reports or tell them what to think. Their individual imaginations and intellects took care of that. They wrote plays, put together costumes from the era, stapled paper together and wrote their own small books, etc.

On occasion, I would have a child write an essay about something they were reading or write up their understanding of Scripture or one of our 24 Family Ways (sometimes as a discipline).

Daily, after our reading time, everyone would disperse to their own corners of the world (bedroom, den with toys, outdoors, etc.) and breathe in the free time they needed to digest all of the input of the reading.

Play is an essential part of ingesting information. When a child gets to romp all over a vast imaginary land and become the hero read about, brain patterns are shaped deeply into the child's psyche. Pretend, dress up, acting out stories—playing deeply solidifies ideas that are rambling in a child's brain from all the stimulation they have received. The mind needs time to rest, to refresh, to restore in order to store up the ideas rolling around. (More about play in chapter 11, on routines.)

Having a good romp outdoors after our reading times gave everyone a time to breathe, to enter into the recesses of their own "mind palace" as Sherlock Holmes suggests. We do not tell our children what to think at this point. We trust them to access the knowledge they have been presented, discussed, understood, and synthesized. Creative outlets of their own making make play an important part of their accessing what they have thought and experienced, giving them time to wonder alone.

Organic, Natural Processes Produce Health and Beauty

Giving room to imagine according to personality and preference meant that each child was shaped by what his or her own mind stored. We plant seeds of thought, ideals, character, faith, philosophy, and the fruit of this planting are crops true, vast, and beautiful.

Our minds and souls were shaped on the same appetites because we invested together in a community of reading and discussing daily for years on end. As my son Nathan commented recently, "We were building our own intimate community, laying lifetime foundations of friendship and co-mentoring."

To teach this way requires a step of faith, leaving behind what is traditional in school systems (including tests and grades); a confident belief that all human beings have a deep desire to learn, to grow, to access ideas and knowledge; and allowing these great ideas to shape who and what they become. The habit of reading daily requires discipline and follow-through. If neglected, mental muscle will be limited, as we were created as people of words.

Often we see extremes in philosophies of education, and we tend to go to one extreme or the other. One side might defend the idea that only strict adherence to formulaic education with a sort of classical or age-graded curriculum will produce the best overall education. You might hear, "Children need to be highly disciplined to access their potential." This implies that the other philosophies of learning are not highly disciplined or effective, which is not true.

> *I have observed some students flourish in all methods and combinations of philosophies, and I have observed some students fail in the same methods when they have not been educated with care and intentionality.*

Then, in a reaction to too much formality, we might be tempted to throw out all of the structure and overemphasize freedom. Letting a child stroke a violin without any instruction or knowledge will produce squeaks and sour strains of notes. Freedom to express comes only after some knowledge is provided as a base.

I have observed some students flourish in all methods and combinations of philosophies, and I have observed some students fail in the same methods when they have not been educated with care and intentionality. Our philosophy was somewhere between total structure and total freedom.

Raising a "Different" Child

"Mama, you will be so surprised at what I have been doing!"

Eleven-year-old Nathan, my third child and second boy, always brought a sparkle to our lives.

With his blueberry eyes, pink and freckled face, and contagious smile, his whole being would light the room and energize the space he occupied. I still wish I could return to those days and live through them again just to see his little-boy, childlike energy bring tap-dancing exuberance to every single moment. How he delighted me, except when he exasperated me.

"What have you been doing?" I asked.

"I have been writing a fantasy novel. I think everyone will love it," he pronounced confidently.

My heart filled with delighted thankfulness. I loved it when Nathan worked hard on something that he had created himself. I had learned that teaching him basics was a bit of a challenge, so I was glad to see him enthusiastic about learning.

Mysterious learning and behavioral issues had created conflict and challenge through our days as I attempted to nurture creativity, intelligence, understanding, skill, and progress to his imagination and to his mind. Spelling was a challenge for him as well as math, and he did not generally punctuate sentences for many years. Details didn't capture his brain's imagination until later. Eventually ADHD, dyslexia, and clinical OCD were some of the labels used to try to get to the bottom of his challenges.

Nathan, though, showed me that there are many kinds of genius. His passion for learning, discussing, debating, and talking about hundreds of ideas helped me to see beyond the boxes that measure education solely by standard testing. I could see amazing attributes through his personality, creativity, and engagement with others.

Now that I understand how brilliant Nathan is, how amazingly he discourses and writes, I see that there was always genius in his mind and heart. His artistic, dynamic personality was not built for conformity, but for expression of great ideas, the broad strokes of intuitive, heartfelt stories. He taught me to think outside the box and to see inside the amazing man God had created him to be.

He taught me that we need to see all people, especially our children, in the context of their own unique design. Then we believe forward in who they will become and seek to provide spaces where they can grow and develop according to their design. (We wrote a book together about our story that might encourage you called *Different: The Story of an Outside-the-Box Kid and the Mom Who Loved Him.*)

For the home-educating parent, the personality, strength, and limitations of children will be constant factors in the learning process, touching on every aspect of family dynamics and child-rearing. How a child lives and learns—and how a parent teaches and trains—will be unavoidably shaped and affected by these issues. Even as we have children with learning disabilities, physical limitations, or spectrum issues, we need to look deep inside at their potential and personality to see how we might strengthen them to have a vibrant life. Development can take many years, so patience is also the grace that paves the way. Looking back, I see that each of my children had their own challenges in different areas.

With everyone at home all the time, though, homeschooling is a laboratory that will give children a tremendous opportunity to test and discover their personality, gifts, potential limitations, and issues that might hinder or enhance their potential. As parents we seek to understand how God has equipped each child to grow fully into their potential and to help them live a purposeful, sustainable life as they merge into adulthood and invest their lives in His kingdom. Being as informed as possible on their individual issues gives hope for the way forward. Life with a child who is different or out of the box brings lots of challenges. Yet educating at home also provides a safe place to develop without criticism or commentary from others.

He taught me foundational truths about seeing each child with an imprint of God on their lives. I learned not to judge or limit the capacity of the child I had been given because he did not fit the norm of learning patterns and styles. I came to understand the importance of seeing into the heart of each child, to imagine with them the possibilities of their own unique story, expression, and call in life.

Nathan would have been labeled by the letters that "experts" used to define some of his seeming issues. Yet God inspired us to minimize the areas where Nathan had difficulty learning or accessing normative test scores. He also helped me to imagine how to develop the areas in which he was strong so that his limitations would not become a disability in his life. This was a long process for our whole family, and yet it helped each of us to grow stronger in character and wisdom.

Nathan had such a vivid imagination. An extensive vocabulary. A heart for heroes and epic tales of adventure and bravery. As an actor, he could move crowds, because he was a power-filled little boy, a pied piper of sorts to other children. They loved him dearly. I could just feel his excitement oozing out.

He loved listening to me read books, and he could discuss ideas brilliantly. So we did much of his work orally, with me sitting next to him and overseeing every part of the curriculum he needed to cover to progress. For instance, he did not capture an understanding of spelling at all until he was in his mid to late teens, when suddenly his brain began to organize letters into proper words much of the time, and he is now the author of six books. Basic math became possible over time, and eventually as an adult, he would even figure out payroll and taxes for the film crews he acquired for his movies.

I do not have space to explain all of the principles I learned by educating Nathan. However, I do want to acknowledge that teaching children with learning or behavioral issues can make life more difficult daily, yearly. So, give yourself grace, find and read about help that addresses your child's needs. But just try to trust God and don't carry stress and worry about things that you cannot immediately change. Nathan excelled beyond my imagination as he authored books, wrote and produced movie scripts, organized movies, and wrote music. All in its time. I see that our uniqueness is something to be celebrated and that seeing each child with possibility and understanding them in context will lay a necessary foundation of unconditional love and acceptance. Some children will be more limited than others, but most children thrive when parents wonder and look for possibilities planted deeply within.

If your child has learning issues, try to look inside to see what areas they are motivated to grow in and emphasize those areas. Get as much input as you can about their particular issues, read up on their areas of struggle, but then apply your own wisdom to your unique child. As a home educator you will be able to more personally give attention to this child's individual needs. All children come with differing personalities, differing motivations and skills, and differing maturity schedules. Learning issues create more stress and pressure for us, the parents, if we assume that all children progress at the same rate and in the same way. Yet if God entrusted these precious ones to us, He will help us find the wisdom to invest in them for their best growth and provide for them to grow as strong and healthy as possible.

The Miracle of Growth

As I see my adult children flourishing, I must say that sometimes I am surprised. The life of our home did not always look like it was producing intelligence, character growth, faith, maturity. Yet when we create a home to meet needs and to enable growth, we will be amazed at the invisible shaping that is taking place in the lives of all growing in the lifegiving environment. It only requires our wonder at the possibilities we cannot see but imagine.

8

Wonderful Moral Muscle: Imagining Character and Virtue

Excellence is an art won by training and habituation: we do not act rightly because we have virtue or excellence, but we rather have these because we have acted rightly . . . we are what we repeatedly do. Excellence, then, is not an act, but a habit.

Will Durant, *The Story of Philosophy*

Educate people without religion and you make them but clever devils.

Attributed to Arthur Wellesley, First Duke of Wellington and former prime minister of England

And not only this, but we also exult in our tribulations, knowing that tribulation brings about perseverance; and perseverance, proven character; and proven character, hope; and hope does not disappoint, because the love of God has been poured out within our hearts through the Holy Spirit who was given to us.

Romans 5:3–5

Hotels have become a very familiar second home to me through many years of traveling and speaking as well as being involved in international ministry in many countries. Recently, while writing this book, I approached this chapter and found myself overwhelmed with many concepts I wanted to cover in so little space. My daughter Joy was spending the night with me in a hotel where I was staying in London. We found ourselves munching on toast, enjoying an omelet, and slowly sipping strong, flat whites. "Joy, I'm writing about character today. Help me limit my ideas and put my finger on what is most important to communicate," I said.

Our conversation about the urgent necessity of providing character training and cultivating responsibility in the lives of children becoming adults in this generation meandered to Augustine, *Jane Eyre*, Superman, and Nazis, where it stayed for a while.

Many of the Nazi officers high up in the regime were well educated, with many holding graduate degrees from well-known universities. Often, while prisoners were being gassed at the concentration camps, opera would be playing and extensive libraries were being enjoyed at the nearby, posh houses of the officers. Many Nazis were highly intellectual and well trained educationally, but their education was mere head knowledge and did not affect their consciences or influence their actions.

What an obvious example of why education cannot be merely cognitive. True education is comprehensive. Learning priorities must include wise insight, biblical conviction, mature models of integrity, and an outworking from the heart, conscience, affections, behavior, and character as well as the mind. Education is not just about facts or philosophy but about the behavior and actions they spawn in one's life.

Though the Nazis were superior in their education, their cleverness made them more "clever devils," as Wellesley said, and with their clever minds they wreaked havoc.

At the end of our conversation, Joy quipped, "Mom, just tell everyone not to raise Nazis."

Character with Academic Excellence

How do we ensure that we do not concentrate so much on the academics that we neglect to build our children's character, inspiring heart, mind, and actions?

We must imagine what it really means to be crafted in the image of God. He is excellent, holy, righteous, and He gives everlasting sacrificial love; He is infinite in knowledge, a creative artist of sublime measure. When we ponder His attributes, we see the potential for us and for our children to become excellent, exceptional, magnificent in growing to reflect His life through ours by actively embodying the character of Christ through our actions. In a culture that exudes mediocrity at every level, we need to push beyond, to live into what our minds can imagine about the greatness of God.

Of course there is great potential, within our extraordinary design, to do evil, to bring darkness and wickedness. And so we arm ourselves with a desire to become the best we can be in every area of our lives and then teach our children from our own integrity. And we teach them to ponder God's attributes and how they are reflected through their world that they might live into His heritage through them.

One afternoon, my son Nathan, a young teenager at the time, was engaged in a book we were reading together about a courageous warrior who died saving friends and others in his city.

"Mama, I bet you have to somehow be trained to be able to fight that well, to have courage to push through all the terrible enemy fire and to have a heart to save others instead of yourself. Courage doesn't usually come out of a vacuum."

As my adult children have forayed into very secular arenas, they have indeed become warriors for righteousness in very dark places. I don't think I even realized how very secular or hard their worlds would be. In their worlds, moral purity is questioned and compromised at every point; traditional views of family, marriage, and the roles of men and women are brought into question. Compromise in virtue (lying, violating moral excellence, blaming others for one's own irresponsibility) is often the standard behavior for many in positions of authority.

Truly, those seeking the best for their students should worry more about giving individual confidence to live a life of exercising moral muscle and virtuous strength than about high academic test scores. Test scores matter not when one creates havoc and chaos in a life untethered to wisdom. Yet I found that when I focused on virtue, my children's test scores and academics were up to par.

It is extremely necessary that we give our children a deeply grounded imagination of what it looks like to be warriors for light, faithful humans in a world of compromise.

Often in education we are straightening a picture on the wall of a house that is burning down. In other words, we can ignore the soul-shaping training that is needful by worrying too much about academic achievement. Education without integrity of life is empty and useless.

It is extremely necessary that we give our children a deeply grounded imagination of what it looks like to be warriors for light, faithful humans in a world of compromise. They need to be able to understand, conceptualize, and practice what they hope to become.

Defining Righteous Moral Character

Righteous moral character can be defined by what a person holds to be good, true, and beautiful that informs their actions. Throughout history, virtues—the values defined by high moral character—have been defined by several lists.

The church fathers defined the virtues as chastity, temperance, charity, diligence, patience, kindness, and humility. There are many lists of virtues. But an important overall umbrella for the different virtues is integrity: having a dependable moral character, a virtuous compass for life.

As believers, we hold that a person's integrity will be based on the model of Christ's life or the fruit of the Spirit found in Galatians 5:22–23. As we place our faith in Christ, He lives through our lives by the Holy Spirit and leads us to live and desire a righteous life, a life of integrity born from His character. Our responsibility is to study His Word and then to ponder how we can please His heart and to capture our children's imagination of what it means to love God with all their heart.

Shaping Character Starts and Ends in Your Child's Heart

So often, the training and discipline of our children focuses on behavior and on control. Capturing their heart with an imagination of why character is important is our goal. One who has grasped a vision for why character matters will be much more likely to pursue what is right than one who is just living by an arbitrary rule. Wonder and imagination play a significant role in shaping character.

Instruction provides a pathway for our children to understand the concepts of character. Modeling from our own lives gives them a pattern to take to heart for what character looks like. Practicing character in daily choices then solidifies what it feels like to act in godly ways. We nurture the formation of character in their hearts through instruction, modeling, and practicing. They merge these truths in their faith-imagination-wonder to form their character.

Character is not just something to be inspired by, but something to see lived out and to practice in order to develop strength of character. It is why we slowly give our children more and more responsibility so that as they learn the basics of virtuous choices, we provide increasingly significant circumstances in which they can practice wise, character-based choices.

We also desire to capture the imagination of *why* strong character matters. Our children must use the moral muscle of their own wonder to understand how character applies. This will influence the decisions they make, the discipline they practice, the perseverance that carries them forward in life. We nurture by reading the stories of people who have lived well. Our children begin to understand the difference godly character can make. They begin to feel and experience the fulfillment of living trustworthy in their own story. We nurture by planting seeds of imagination that reflect the value of character.

Peter, the one who was nurtured in his faith by Jesus, shows the power of nurture in the opening words of his second pastoral letter (see 2 Peter 1:3–11). It was written to adults, but the truths and principles can apply directly to parents and their children, as do the two resulting promises that every Christian parent wants to claim for their children.

Peter starts by declaring that we have everything we need for "life and godliness" and that it is found in Christ (v. 3). It is all given so that we can "participate in the divine nature" (v. 4 NIV) and experience the life of God. That is all the language of nurture. Then Peter describes the process that will enable any person to find that life. He offers not just random qualities and commitments, but a progressive picture of biblical nurture.

Faith is the foundation upon which everything else will be built, and each quality builds on the one before it. This is how biblical nurture should work. To faith, add

goodness—because faith leads to pursuing morality and goodness,

knowledge—because goodness leads to desiring more divine truth,

self-control—because truth leads to exercising more self-control,

perseverance—because self-control leads to the need to persevere,

godliness—because perseverance leads to pursuing godliness,

brotherly kindness—because godliness leads to fellowship (*philia* love), and

love—because fellowship leads to unconditional love (*agape* love).

If you, as a Christian parent, are growing in these qualities and you are adding them to your children's lives in order to nurture the life of Christ in them, Peter lets you know that you can claim two promises. First, these qualities will keep you and your children "from being ineffective and un-productive" in your knowledge of Christ (v. 8 NIV).

As you nurture your children and impart the life of Christ to them, you can be assured that they will grow in their spiritual maturity. Second, these qualities come with the promise that "if you do these things, you will never stumble, and you will receive a rich welcome into the eternal kingdom of our Lord and Savior Jesus Christ" (v. 10–11 NIV). Although every child will grow by learning how to overcome temptation and sin, no godly parent ever wants their children to have to learn from failure that leads to a fall. Peter is saying that when you add the seven qualities and virtues to your children's faith, you are strengthening them so they will not fall into a pattern of sin or fall away from God. That is a biblical promise to pursue!

Empowering Children to Imagine Their Own Godly Character

We wanted to empower our children to take responsibility for their own lives, understanding that their choices would have consequences. Children learn to work by doing chores, completing tasks, serving others. They learn to have integrity by learning to tell the truth, to be dependable, to cultivate trustworthiness. Our desire in training is to help our children develop their own agency in making choices, exercising godliness.

We always said, "We cannot make you strong inside or virtuous of character. But you have the ability to choose to practice being strong by learning to practice the ways of God."

Training in character gives our children the foundation of internal strength to learn responsibility and the motivation to be able to do what God has prepared them to do in life. To focus merely on knowledge without laying a foundation of character makes education limited and without purpose. Training children to grow the muscle of character prepares them to be able to apply the knowledge, skills, and wisdom they have learned in practical ways.

Their learning that they were the stewards of telling a good life story meant we needed to prepare them to value and practice character habits so they would know how to make decisions when they forayed out into a world filled with distractions and temptations. As I have said many times, in the absence of biblical convictions, people will go the way of their culture and cultural voices. We wanted them to have another voice inside their mind, convictions that would guide them in how to make wise decisions, how to cultivate godly character.

As an aside, our family used the *Our 24 Family Ways* family devotional guide that my husband, Clay, wrote to address six areas of family life: authority, relationships, possessions, work, attitudes, and choices. The 24 Family Ways helped us teach biblical principles, create a common language, and provide some objective standards of behavior for cultivating godliness for our family. They allowed us to avoid nagging and to focus more on positive training. Each Family Way also has a related character quality and a Scripture memory verse.

This material became the basis for our children to understand the ways of God in their lives.

We often quoted Proverbs 4:18: "But the path of the righteous is like the light of dawn, that shines brighter and brighter until the full day." Our children were on a pathway of becoming mature and strong of faith, so with each year they would grow in wisdom and in faith and reflect more of the light of God in each step of their life journey.

Little ones need the grace that allows them to be immature and childish while growing little by little toward maturity. It takes a lifetime to become mature. One little step at a time.

Walking with the Wise, Avoiding Foolish Companionship

Memorizing some passages that were visual in nature gave us a form on which to hang the concept of developing moral muscle. We then used Psalm 15 as a picture of seeking to be in God's inner circle of those closest to His heart.

> O Lord, who may abide in Your tent?
> Who may dwell on Your holy hill?

> He who walks with integrity, and works righteousness,
> And speaks truth in his heart.
>
> vv. 1–2

Walking shows a picture of moving through life day by day, year by year. Walking with integrity as a grid through which we want to make decisions helped our children retain a mental image of every day living life with integrity (being whole, dependably honest, upright, virtuous in words and deeds).

A person's character can be seen in who they imagine themselves to be inside. Wholeness and moral goodness that is exercised when no one is looking—what they do in secret when they have no accountability—proves a heart that embraces personal integrity. In other words, good character is not about performance in front of people but about how a person behaves from the values he holds fast in his heart, all the time, in every situation. Cultivating the wonder of what it would look like to be a virtuous person meant we would ask questions: "How does a virtuous person behave?" "Can you think of an example from a story or from your own life?" "What does it look like to be courageous, truthful, to make good moral choices, to be loyal, faithful, etc.?"

We had a grid throughout our lives together for searching out stories that showed ways in which people behaved virtuously and places where integrity was uncompromised so that our children could store up examples for when they were up against similar choices or temptations.

Several concepts or terms helped to build the sense of a virtuous self. Wide parameters of time and freedom provided grace to learn to act out these concepts in real life. Walking beside them as they grew and giving direction and encouragement as mentors helped them to develop their own moral muscle.

Concepts to Fuel Ownership of a Strong Moral Character

Self-government

Just knowing the definition of some words provides vision and direction in life. So it is with the concept of self-government. To govern oneself is basically the idea of using self-control, self-discipline, or self-order. It empowers children to understand that they have the ability, the power, to rule over who they become, to determine what they become. Self-government gives them a sense of ownership over the destiny of their lives.

We used this idea often in our child training, as vocabulary helps a child to develop a proper sense of self.

"You have a potential for growing strong inside, to develop character muscle. You can be strong in love, courage, diligence—all the attributes that are good—but you have to decide that it is what you want to do. We can encourage you and help you, but you are the one who needs to learn to rule over all the areas of your life that you want to be strong in so that you can become the best person you imagine being. Your choices will have consequences. If you make good choices, your life will grow in wisdom. If you refuse to act wisely, you will have to accept the negative consequences of your choice as your own responsibility."

> *It empowers children to understand that they have the ability, the power, to rule over who they become, to determine what they become.*

A point of wonder might be to imagine the role of a king. Jesus uses the picture of Him being a king and ruling in His kingdom. We might say, "Even as a king rules over his people and his kingdom, so you will rule over your own self, your sphere of influence, your talents and resources to bring about goodness in the pathways of your life. What you practice determines who you become. What would it look like to have a good king? How would he exhibit good character? What would the attributes of a bad king be? What would be the effects of that ruler's poor decisions on his kingdom?"

Agency and will

Agency is the power that a person has to act or make decisions on their own behalf. Helping our children know that they must engage in life and make decisions for themselves to chart the course of their lives creates strength and maturity. The will is the determination of choosing how one will act. They can choose to obey instruction or disobey. They can choose to study for a test, pay their bills, show up for a commitment, be a good friend, or not. Helping our children understand this idea was to help them imagine that inside themselves they would be making decisions big and small the rest of their lives by exerting their will—deciding how they would make a decision. Instead of letting them be controlled by a desire to please us, we freed them to understand the responsibility and freedom they had to chart their own course.

In a world where many blame others for the circumstances of their lives, giving a child an understanding of agency empowers them to know that they have the ability to overcome difficulties, to create harmony in relationships, to work hard to achieve their goals. These outcomes are a matter of using their agency and exerting their will.

Speaking Forward into the Person a Child Is Becoming

Often we talked to our children about imagining what it meant to be a hero. We explained that a hero often faces the same circumstances of life that many others face, but the hero is the one who steps out in courage, takes a risk to work harder, has an inner value of protecting others. Being courageous, dependable, or steadfast is a decision of their inside self that results in an outside action.

The motivation comes from the imagination and determination of who he is called to be. *You have a will inside your heart. It is the part of you that decides to make good decisions or give in to temptation. By using your will, you can decide to work hard or to be lazy.* In other words, the outcome of your life, the process of reaching your potential, is contained in your decision, your agency, to do an action or to practice a good habit of life. What you practice, you will become; if you decide to tell the truth or admit you made a mistake, even if it has consequences, you have exercised your will to be honest and to please God. Each of us has vast potential and capacity, but we are the ones who determine how much we will apply ourselves to access that potential.

"We hope you will be a hero in the story of your life and give your life to goodness, love, helping others, because that will take you on a pathway of favor and grace. We cannot make you do that—you have to decide it for yourself. You have a will, the ability to make a decision about all the details of your life. We can teach you the best things we know, but only you can decide to follow them and act on them," we explained.

Giving children a vocabulary about character and faith, agency and will so that they can refer to it as they begin to develop their own muscle and have a way to go forward offers them a sort of self-power. We were made to grow in virtue and to be satisfied in our souls by learning to be righteous (to act rightly). We help our children become satisfied in life when we equip them with these virtues.

In a culture that gives permission to individuals to blame others for their own bad behavior, we need to help our children understand that they are responsible for their actions, their behavior. Each must exercise their will, the ability to decide what to do in all circumstances and relationships, for the good. A life of integrity, being steadfast in exercising virtuous character, is being trustworthy and true and dependable in life.

Capacity and Potential

Within the beautiful design of being human, each of us is given great capacity, a broad space for developing our moral muscle, our moral strength, our ability to work hard. We also have capacity to think, create, do inventive works. But even as it requires resistance and exertion to build strong bodily muscles, it requires an exercise of our will to grow into our capacity and potential for becoming fruitful and productive in every area of life.

Even as our bodies can become exhausted and resist exercise, so our wills can be depleted and we become tempted to resist hard work, faithfulness, diligence. But holding a value for godly character (loyalty, diligence, faithfulness) can push us toward reaching our capacity and potential.

As one in my sixties, I am continually amazed at what, by God's grace, I was able to do. Often, I would be in challenging circumstances and think, *I don't know if I am going to make it! I feel like my life is demanding too much from me.* I was without a good support system, moving nineteen times, seven times internationally; keeping up with four children, two of them clinically obsessive compulsive and one with learning issues; and carrying a full load of work, combined with the normal stresses of life. Sometimes I wondered if it was too much, if I could even keep going. And yet, I would take one day at a time, make one more step forward, and seek to be faithful in that day.

Eventually I could look back and see that I had much more capacity than I thought to work diligently, to love more unconditionally, to persevere in challenging circumstances, and to cultivate my faith even in dark times. God stretched my muscle to show me He made me with great capacity. By His grace, I found I was able to accomplish much more than I could have ever imagined. Was it challenging and hard? Of course, but I got stronger and stretched my capacity to be faithful every year as I learned and exercised these concepts, because I had no other choice.

It took me years and years to understand how far I could stretch myself. I was sorely tempted many times to give up my ideals because of discouragement, wondering if my effort was making any difference. Bouts of depression accompanied many seasons. Exhaustion tempted me to quit. And seeming failures along the way caused me to worry if I was enough for my tasks. But I learned little by little to walk faithfully toward the burdens of my work, and the result is that my ability to work and to push through became stronger. I would have learned wisdom for life much earlier if I had been instructed and trained or had a mentor who taught and showed me the meaning of potential.

In light of our own experience of "pushing further, working a little bit more," we learned to help our children strive for excellence, complete tasks, do their work as excellently as possible. All of us have more capacity than we imagine. But we must embrace a vision for our potential strength and then use our agency to make decisions in attempting to work toward our goals and ideals day after day. In doing so, we become a living model to our children of what great integrity and virtue, and living into our potential, look like in the trenches of life.

Now, because of practice in our home, my adult children have tackled difficult and idealistic goals. We walk along and encourage them, help them when there is a practical need. We encourage them to grow in their own capacity, believing with them that they can make it through challenging tasks, one step at a time.

Each child has great capacity for growth, strength, virtuous character. They will be more likely to exercise more of their capacity if we speak to them of their ability to access their potential, and then allow them to make their own decisions to grow and make commitments and become strong inside and out.

When children are small, you protect, instruct, love, model. Don't pressure your children toward performance, especially when they are just learning, playing, pretending, laying foundations. Let them have the gift of being innocent children. Then, little by little, as they grow older, you expand their responsibilities and decision making while they are still with you so that you can support them.

Motivating children to make and fulfill their own goals keeps them from living by performance for us, their parents. We focus on what matters (all human beings, meeting their needs, relationships, family, love, serving others) instead of focusing on public achievement or accomplishment. In a world that measures success by money, power, and influence, we emphasize those accomplishments that are holistic, healthy, humane. You will see a gradual turning from childishness to moving in the direction of adulthood. When they grow older, you gently give more and more responsibility and freedom as they show capability. Let them commit to real responsibilities outside of your home and influence: jobs, projects, creative ventures, volunteer work. Then support them. Controlling a child's decisions or life never builds strength.

Often, as parents or teachers we want to retrieve our children from difficult or challenging circumstances. Yet the only way muscle is built is by pushing against resistance or pressure. Learning when not to save my children from potentially difficult circumstances took prayer and searching for wisdom. Letting them feel the consequences of life but walking beside them in encouragement meant they grew in character and insight.

Of course, we must be sensitive to age, capacity, and circumstance and not push our little ones into a strenuous situation. Children need the gift of innocence as long as possible. There are always unavoidable challenges in each of our lives. I can see so much better that it was the difficulties our family faced and pushed through by faith over the years that helped our adult children know what it looks like to become overcomers. All became warriors for righteousness, and they learned to be steadfast in their own ideals and circumstances when they left home because they saw what it looked like in real life. Being controlling or overprotective of children can cause them to be ill prepared as adults for the battles they will certainly face.

Creating a Vision to Live On Purpose

"Living on purpose" was a phrase that we articulated often. You may recognize this as a repeated theme in this book. God ordained that we become partners in bringing His light to a dark world. He sent His disciples out into the world to "make disciples," followers of Christ and worshippers of God. When we fulfill our destiny by living on purpose for what matters, we find soul satisfaction that can never be gained through money or status.

Even as our own heavenly Father determined to allow us to be a part of His work of redeeming the world, we understand that our children were made to be a part of a movement bigger than themselves and they long for their lives to have purpose and meaning.

Foundational to passing on character and inspiring wonder in how they would live a life of integrity was communicating to them that they had a story to tell. Their stories would be determined by the ways that they lived faithfully in their lifetimes. Passing on a personal vision to each of them meant that they left our home owning their own faith, their own call to bring God's light and truth to their world.

Provide many opportunities for your family to live on purpose by serving others. For us, it began with our women's conferences where each of us served for more than twenty years. It also included mission trips; serving in a soup kitchen; hosting speakers, musicians, or missionaries; hosting parties for all ages of kids; hosting a Bible study in our home; teaching classes; making meals for neighbors; serving at conferences or volunteering at a historical house; baby-sitting children from other families; helping people move; etc. There are endless ways to serve, but practicing service as a family lays foundations in your children's imagination that they are those who give and serve.

Preparing for Conflict

Jesus never promised His disciples an easy life but prepared them to bring light into darkness. And so we sought to arm our children, to prepare them to become warriors for righteousness and love.

Instead of trying to shield our children from all difficulties, when life brought challenges and worldly exposure to our children, we walked with them through it. Talking to them about the issues they would encounter prepared them to face the world and its struggles and temptations when they left our home. All subjects they wanted to discuss were fair game, as we wanted to be the ones who informed their morals, values, ideas.

Jesus said, "Behold, I send you out as sheep in the midst of wolves; so be shrewd as serpents and innocent as doves" (Matthew 10:16). And so we taught them to imagine what it would feel like, look like, to be disappointed, discouraged, weary and what it would take to keep going forward. Faith, as in Hebrews 11:6, is the engine with which we drive forward in challenging circumstances. Faith moves us forward in our actions. "Faith is the assurance of things hoped for, the conviction of things not seen" (Hebrews 11:1). Understanding that their virtuous choices matter, that hard work will pay off, that faithfulness in relationship will help them ultimately to grow gave forward motion to their own dreams and goals.

As our children become adults, they have to learn to work in spite of the pressures of their jobs. Imagine the life of a heart surgeon or a critical care nurse, or a factory worker, a teacher, a pastor or missionary, a composer, a farmer. Each of these professions is worthy. But each job is loaded with stress, pressure, problems. It is only the one who learns to push through the problems who will continue to reap a salary. Quitting often limits our ability to see a good ending play itself out over time.

Endless Possibilities

There is an infinite number of areas in which we could teach and pass on concepts of character. If children wonder what these examples might look like in their own lives, they will be better prepared to know how to tackle the difficulties as adults. To teach our children the value of moral muscle and the place of faith is to arm them with the defenses they will need to access their potential and capacity and to live a life of integrity. In teaching them and taking responsibility to mentor them to become strong, we also learn more about living into our own capacity. Our children stretch our ability and capacity to grow our whole lives.

Motivating children to make
and fulfill their own goals
keeps them from living
by performance for us,
their parents.

9

Creating Wonder-Filled Culture Shapers

Culture: The art, music, literature, and all creative expressions that embody and express the traditions and values of peoples and countries to reflect a picture of their celebrations and beliefs unique to their place and history.

Human creativity, then, images God's creativity when it emerges from a lively, loving community of persons and, perhaps more important, when it participates in unlocking the full potential of what has gone before and creating possibilities for what will come later.

> Andy Crouch, *Culture Making:*
> *Recovering Our Creative Calling*

In the beginning God created.

> Genesis 1:1

The chill late October wind stormed against us, bringing tears to my eyes. Wild waves swept across the ocean horizon, back and forth, rhythmically pouring out the music of the arriving stormy blast. Huddled together, sitting on a rickety bench placed strategically on the edge of the grassy cliff, I nestled close to my daughter and son as we quietly pondered all that had previously lived in this place.

At our backs, old cathedral ruins filled with gravestones whispered to us of mysteries, the religious battles of those who had gone before. Stories of priests and monks, fathers and mothers, children and friends who had weathered the storms of life together in this old Scottish cathedral filled our imaginations.

Thousands had made a pilgrimage here to St. Andrews to offer their hopes, fears, weariness, desires, and prayers. History records that violent arguments arose over doctrinal convictions. The sacred cathedral that had been a balm, a place where love was given and shelter provided to tens of thousands, was destroyed in clashes over God's reputation and nature. Huge carved-stone spires stood boldly in defiance of the brazen wind, and the remains of the cathedral design stood fast, as if to say, "My purpose will not be forgotten, my protection still stands for those who would seek refuge in this place."

The wildness of the winds, the power of sacred voices seemed to sweep the murkiness and contamination of hurry off my soul. I slowly released my inner self into the steadfast strength of the place that had not abandoned its meaning or purpose through the centuries.

Later, as we meandered through the vast grounds of the ruins together, Joel and Joy conversed about the history of this sacred place. The story made the burial grounds come alive to me. Reading some of the hundreds of tombstones, knowing that all who had lived before me in this place had lived a story well or badly, reminded me of my own transient, temporal, brief life. Desires to be faithful with the time I have been given were spurred.

Soon, a cafe called our names as it promised warm respite. Speaking to one another of the impact of the grand cathedral, even on our own lives today, spawned a greater conversation. Each spoke of many places we had traveled to over the years where the culture, the art, the music, the stories of sites we studied and visited had shaped our own vision. We learned what was possible for us to invest in through our lifetime as the ancient stories catalyzed our personal goals and life work. Experiences like this one filled our imaginations as memories were stored in each place we visited.

As evidence to the testimony of cultural creativity, these two, Joel and Joy, had engaged in the rigorous work of completing a PhD in the theology of imagination and the arts so that they could become culture creators in their vocations and lives. Sarah had become a teller of tales and an exhorter of great ideas. Nathan decided to shape stories through movies and books.

The significance of remembering history and pondering the legacy of great stories and messages of the past drives us forward to carry a legacy of courage and truth to our generation. Imagination of what others' lives have provided for us through their faithfulness spawns strength and courage to live our own stories, to invest in the thread of human love, courage, and faith.

Years of swimming in story, music, theology, art, architecture, horticulture, gardening, movies, children's dramas, theater, photography, various plays and musicals, etc. had planted an interest to pursue teaching, writing, and inspiring others to comprehend the impact of culture on life and faith issues. Those who shape and cultivate cultural messages bring great sway and influence to their worlds.

Our conversation led us to remember a visit to a home in Illinois designed by architect Frank Lloyd Wright, where nature was invited into each room in the house; our first time attending the musical *Les Misérables* in Colorado and being changed by enchanting music and the story of sacrifice and love amid a time of war; studying and seeing through the public library the renderings of the impressionist paintings of French artists whose works expressed a different way of seeing light; listening to classical music through the centuries and getting to know the stories and countries of various composers right in our living room; and how *December*, composed by George Winston, brought us comfort in the cold Colorado winters, and still did today in Scotland.

Exposing my children to a vast smorgasbord of culture expressed through art, music, theater, architecture, history, and travel was one of the most profoundly influential foundations for their intellect, faith, and engagement in academics. *Art and culture express the heartbeat of people as a bookmark of history.*

Cultural events are what helped to equip my children to prepare for college, to be able to write papers, to debate well. An understanding of the humanities prepares us to think, to synthesize knowledge, to articulate wisdom from the context of real-life philosophies. And instead of just memorizing dates and facts, culture immersion creates a depth of understanding and a world vocabulary.

People all over the world write to me asking how to best prepare a young adult to do well on their pre-entrance exams for university. Contemporary education has convinced us that real learning involves primarily studying to a test, covering only certain subjects, and focusing on right answers in textbooks and precollege tests. By age seventeen, many teens (and their teachers) are disinterested in learning or in studying life in the way I described.

True education is beyond tests, grades, and standardized measurement. Education isn't about making sure your children learn a list of facts and figures. It's not about a score on a test or a letter on a paper. It's about informing young souls in a way that shapes and inspires them to live into the story God has for their life.

Once our children turned sixteen, we inaugurated each into their own course of study based on their personal interests and possible future professions, involving more of their individual engagement. Perhaps teens are bored in high school because sometimes it is boring and pedantic in nature, perhaps requiring little of their ability to engage, to think, to explore ideas and philosophy.

Yet, learning how to think, to understand the rise and fall of civilizations, the reflection of a culture's history through its art and culture, develops deeply intellectual people. Exercising the mind in thought, philosophy, history, and concepts of culture can seem superfluous to those studying for college entrance exams.

Yet, when we submerge ourselves in vastly important thought life, the natural consequence is that test taking is accomplished more easily. All of my children did well on their college entrance tests and in real-life endeavors and garnered scholarships as needed. But if a child is not raised to think and dive into the context of a culture and understand peoples and philosophy from the beginning, it will be hard to develop that muscle the year before college exams must be taken. I hate to keep using this word, but reductive education teaches to the test, is often soul-deadening, and is one-dimensional. Wonder-filled learning sharpens minds, builds intellect and intelligence, sparks interest, and provides great insight into life.

Movies, literature, television, music, art, architecture, horticulture, and scientific discoveries that shaped the world reflect the souls of people and provide the meaning and context of government, politics, wars, religions, and behavior. People think and value life in particular ways because of the messages and artifacts that have surrounded them.

Cultural themes provide not only insight into a time in history, but also give joy, create convictions, show values, inspire our decisions, and create a desire for purpose and influence. Ancient stories and courageous actions of real people throughout history hold us accountable to live our lives well, in the context of the times we have been given. Remembering what has gone before inspires us to act with integrity for what is ahead in our own lives and decisions.

> *Cultural themes provide not only insight into a time in history, but also give joy, create convictions, show values, inspire our decisions, and create a desire for purpose and influence.*

Traveling to experience historical homes, battlegrounds, art galleries, science museums shapes a wonder-filled imagination with dimension, creativity, and desire. Even if you cannot travel widely, every area has within a couple of hundred miles museums, concerts, plays, historical ruins. The Internet is filled with resources and documentaries. There are movies and traveling theaters to provide opportunities for immersion in cultural pursuits. People are more shaped today by television, movies, and music than ever before. To understand this and to be a culture shaper means one can influence culture by crafting poignant messages creatively.

Bear with me as I write a bit about philosophy of life and why beauty, color, creativity matter. Faith issues and worship are tied to understanding the vast importance of culture.

Recognizing the Creativity of God

Diversity of every kind is expressed in the art of God as found in our world. His created elements are reflected in our everyday life. We live by the reflection of the colors of the sun and clouds, mountains and rivers that our eyes behold wherever we live. The color and texture of the food we eat (American comfort, Mexican, Italian, Middle Eastern, Asian) is from a combination of various spices, herbs, meats, and veggies He designed. We experience and enjoy through our taste buds multiple times each day. The clothes and styles we wear, with jewelry adornments, convey the valuing of design, comfort, and personal expression. The colors of the walls of our homes and the photographs or art that we have on display reflect the color God created. The music we buy and listen to with the ears God has given us broadens our imagination as well. Culture is an art form that each human being expresses through what they choose to celebrate and value as a reflection of being made in the image of God, the first and ultimate creator.

The aesthetic pleasure of diving into cultural experiences increases happy hormones in our brains—and it is just a lot of fun. "Human creativity, then, images God's creativity," as Andy Crouch writes.[1] Movies, literature, culinary arts, garden selection and design, decorating a home or space, and music give energetic life to our imaginations.

God was first an innovative creator, and we, made in His image, are also co-creators. We use the raw materials of life, personality, preference, and imagination to create our own unique expressions of beauty and color through many differing mediums. And in creating our own, we can understand different cultures and expand our view of the world by observing and contrasting other unique cultural creations. A world that sees, experiences, and values cultural experiences validates the overarching manifestation of God's original role as artist. It also calls us, as a reflection of Him, to become artists in our domains.

Multidimensional reflections within the expression of His personality and creation help us to understand that, like God, we are multidimensional. We live fully when we exercise our minds, bodies, souls, emotions, wills, and creativity.

Touring an art gallery, we might admire a particular painting or sculpture and recognize the subject as something that appeals to us, or understand it as a reflection of a time in history, or enjoy the light and colors.

When we take time to appreciate design we are called deeply into experiencing the joy of life. The cold of a snowflake, the elegance of a swan gliding over water, and the delight at seeing thousands of birds flying in unison in a perfect V while sounding out their voices in squawks and quacks call us to merely engage in the beautiful. Beauty is of great soul and mind value in and of itself.

God, and even basic knowledge, is not just a cognitive, pedantic thought or philosophy to understand. Instead, God has personality, love, emotion, affection, artistic expression that we observe to understand Him and to know His infinite capacity, which leads us to worship Him. And when we create and design, we are reflecting Him and understanding Him better in and through our own experience.

I was riding in a train once after I had been on a mission trip in five countries, experiencing a variety of food, clothing, and customs. All were quite foreign to my own preferences. I suddenly had the thought that God could easily relate to the people whose customs and habits were so different from mine and realized that God was not primarily American in His preferences. This may seem obvious, but to experience it personally—not just as a thought but as a reality—changed how I felt about people from different cultural backgrounds who experienced different cultural pressures and political oppression.

This understanding made me realize that He is much bigger than my tiny little perspective. To understand the personality of God, we must seek to understand other peoples, languages, historical contexts, customs, ways of expressing faith. Studying culture expands our knowledge, our interest in philosophy, our experience in political issues, our depth of seeing life as nuanced by historical occurrences.

The Deep Influence of Culture

Proper culture shaping, then, reflects our creative response to life in mirroring His creativity through us. Throughout each span of time, the music and folk songs, the literature and stories passed down, the works of art, tapestries, stained-glass windows, wood carvings, architecture, feasts, traditions tell the stories of the heart issues of each place. They leave a trail of what each people celebrated and held dear.

Becoming shapers of culture and art helps us to resist submitting to worldly values or blindly accepting them. Diving into culture and appreciating diversity shows us the way to live beyond the conformity of peer pressure and bias. If our goal is to help our children become strong in thought, we must give them a depth of understanding of those who have shaped culture as well as the ability to interpret the messages shaped by artists and those who reflected values through what they created.

Unfortunately, social media influencers are pervasively responsible for shaping our own contemporary culture and values. We often just sit back and accept the messages that movies, television, music, creative arts, and consumerism dictate to us to believe and adopt as our own values. These messages reflect the soul of what is believed and embraced and valued in our world today. To ignore the themes of contemporary movies, music, and art is to put our heads in the sand, refusing to engage in what is on the hearts and in the minds of our contemporaries. To reach and extend wisdom and understanding to people different from us, we must learn to see others in the context of their expressed needs and thoughts.

Shaping the wonder of our children to imagine making artifacts of creativity that might shape a generation is a worthy exercise. Technology tends toward dehumanization and deconstructing individual expression unless it is used to expand creativity, human value, community. Utilitarianism and practicality are often valued above beauty. To devalue beauty and design is to diminish what God created the world to be as a reflection of His personality and creative intellect. To depersonalize God by valuing technology, utilitarianism, and efficiency as the highest assets creates disconnection from our souls and produces a one-dimensional life, with little value for the humane.

In a time that places technological achievements and utilitarianism above the mystery of sublime design, creativity, the soul filling of music and story, we must shape our children's appetites and wonder on aesthetic beauty and challenge them to consider how they might shape or make culture.

By celebrating the reflection of individual artistic endeavor we touch their hearts, not just their minds. Sending them into their world as human beings who have been influenced by the imaginary, the wonder of life will help keep souls alive and minds fresh with possibility. Culture making is about heart shaping, not just measurable accomplishment.

Ancient history shows us that skilled craftsmen carved wooden furniture and shaped panels on walls from diverse wood. Artisans imagined exquisite tapestries that filled the walls of castles. Marble statues were shaped to make the images of historical figures come to life. Oil paintings give us remnants of the homes, countryside, dress, and people of other times. To imagine life throughout the centuries through culture observed is to build a robust understanding of ideas and values.

Now much of our work is digital, administrative, and devoid of emotion, which can dehumanize inner selves. When color, beauty, crafting, creativity are absent from life, souls lose consciousness for tradition, rituals, and symbols. The end result is colorless, emotionless, spiritless life. One house looks like the next; one person acts like the rest. Beauty and creativity keep our souls' imagination of faith, God, and the universe alive.

Imagine a Thanksgiving meal prepackaged by the hundreds with many preservatives and chemicals, factory produced. The result is unhealthy consumption of mass-produced food. Compare that to a fresh, organic feast with unprocessed turkey basting in the oven, grandma's dressing recipe made from real ingredients, salads of greens, and a variety of veggies, fruit, and nuts, homemade pumpkin pies with fresh whipped cream (not from a can), and multigrain yeast rolls that rose earlier in the day, freshly made from milled grain.

> Beauty and creativity keep our souls' imagination of faith, God, and the universe alive.

We have become used to a prepackaged, factory-results sort of education that minimizes quality when we were created for fresh, human-crafted, and human-imagined recipes for life that are beautiful to see as well as flavorful to experience. The same with art and culture: Our souls become diminished, dry, and lifeless when we reduce life to what can be measured by expediency.

Cultural expressions of art reflect the creative God within us. For me as a co-artist with God, understanding that I was made in His image meant I could reflect Him by creating my own museum of cultural artifacts. I filled our home with reminders of created art in differing styles, including Polish wooden boxes and figurines from my years of living in Kraków and Warsaw that were carved by craftsmen in a wooded region of the country. Green chile chicken enchiladas graced our table, gleaned from living on the border of Mexico in Texas as a child and falling in love with the spicy food of that region. A secondhand Austrian pottery set was used on holidays, and stories were remembered from times in missions there. English china teacups (because china keeps tea hotter longer) were collected from garage sales and secondhand stores over time, because I had grown up with such cups at my grandmother's kitchen table and they spoke to us of our English heritage.

Numbered prints by artists we knew lined our walls. Calligraphy of favorite verses and sayings influenced the thoughts and preferences of all of us as we passed by them each day. We became culture creators ourselves because we were immersed in the color, beauty, and enjoyment of it surrounding us every day.

Cultural Expressions at Home: More Specifics

Art

Collecting art books full of every genre of art and displaying them in baskets all over the house ensured that, at any spare moment, we would all be flipping through the varied and colorful expressions of artists preserved through time and across cultures.

Small easels bought at a craft store provided a place where I could display art or photography all through the house as a validation of what we could observe, appreciate, enjoy.

Before Clay and I were married and after, we collected and framed small pieces of art from friends who painted. We also chose unique pieces from different cities all over the world where we have lived that were symbolic of images we learned to love. All of our children have begun to collect their own art that reflects their unique personalities and preferences. These pieces now cover their walls, mantles, shelves, tables.

Calligraphy is a beautiful and old expression of lettering reflecting an ancient art form to give value to important words. Collecting Scripture that was illuminated by a favorite artist in the old European style meant that on anniversaries, we would buy one more verse to place on our walls. Discussing the verses, observing the colors, pondering the meanings, and then hanging them in our rooms meant that the messages subtly entered our own places of wonder and imagination.

Photography

A collection of devotional books that are reflective of the photographic splendor of nature (the wilds of Africa, famous mountains, sunrises, flowers, thunderclouds, etc.) all over the world became a favorite that

I read from at mealtime or placed on an easel in sight or used during devotions.

Myriads of photographs of our family in memorable moments or places together adorn tabletops, shelves, and walls to commemorate that we are a community of love, that we have fun together, celebrate together, and walk through storms together.

Music

Because Clay and I were both musicians of sorts, we took great pleasure in exposing our children to many different forms of music. I grew up playing piano, sang in all-state choirs, and performed in contemporary bands from high school through the early years of our marriage; Clay is a singer-songwriter who has written hundreds of songs and performed throughout our whole life together.

Daily, as I got out of bed, I would move toward the teakettle and also put on some kind of music. Clay gave each of us small speakers that we could connect to our phones so we could have high-quality sound in our rooms! Christian artists and acoustic musicians we all loved traveled with us through mountain trips as we belted out familiar and favorite songs.

Acoustic CDs became my favorite for daily playing, because I found music with lyrics a distraction when I was trying to read aloud or have a discussion. Celtic artists, beautiful movie themes, classical pieces, acoustic guitarists, cello, and violin were just a few of our favorites.

Contemporary singer-songwriters filled our home and car through hours and hours. James Taylor helped me to teach Joy to drive as his music calmed us both during the sixty hours of practice driving she had to complete for her driver's license. Music was our comfort, inspiration, and pleasurable experience every day.

Concerts and performances were attended as often as we could afford or as often as someone worth seeing came to town. Appreciating the highlights of the *Messiah* by Handel was a yearly activity. Knowing the story of Handel as a popular composer in his lifetime, as popular as any musician today, captured the imagination of everyone. Knowing that he sequestered himself for three weeks almost without sleeping or eating and wrote out thousands and thousands of notes for vocal soloists and an orchestra with a rapturous libretto (the words) fascinated us all.

Reading passages of Isaiah aloud, we would imagine the God who spoke tenderly through the hauntingly beautiful melodies we listened to at mealtime. Reflecting on the story passed down about English King George standing in honor of the "Hallelujah Chorus" reminded us that there was a sense of honor and respect for worthy performances in other generations. When we took our children to live performances, Handel's *Messiah* was a story they had heard about, by a composer with a real personality they knew of, based on passages written by an ancient prophet with whom they had become familiar. All listened intently for the "Hallelujah Chorus" so they could be the first to stand. In other words, it was not just another "boring" classical performance, but they were familiar with the story, the time, the prophet, the composer, and the king. (There's so much more to the story, but you get the idea.)

I couldn't have known back then that I was planting seeds of creativity in the imagination of one of my children, who would himself become a composer of choral music, film scores, and original music, but he (Joel) says it happened while falling in love with the expansive influence of music on our lives over time.

Horticulture and gardening, floral arrangement

Favorite places to visit over the years were the botanical gardens in each large city we visited or lived near. From Japanese gardens to exquisite floral displays and vast arrays of autumn leaves, our senses were delighted just by our walking, observing, breathing in the beauty. How specifically each plant was planted, groomed, placed for the climates unique to it entered our conversations.

Harvest times often led us to visit farms with pumpkins, apples, and berries to pick and hay rides to enjoy. We would find places in the regions we lived in and keep up with carnivals or picking seasons. Seeing the hard work of subduing, planting, watering, and protecting gave us a picture of God's care for us in a different way.

Travel

Because I was sometimes bored and restless (I was the original ADD person in our family, and I am a visionary/intuitive person by personality), I loved exploring the world with my family. I wanted them to have a "world" view of life that included experiencing cultures, art, and beauty by engaging in traditions and celebrations from many cultures over many centuries.

Because of my own young-adult life as a missionary, traveling in many countries, I planned and discovered ways to travel cheaply. We found deals on the Internet, rented Airbnbs, and piled all six of us into a hotel room with sleeping bags on the floor. Often, I would write ahead on personal social media and ask if there were any people living in a certain area for specific input about what to see and experience in their region. Many, many times, people offered to have us stay with them and to be our tour guides. Of course, we filtered the invitations, but some of our dear friendships, to this day, came from such generous offers of hospitality that led to our children interacting and making friends. It also provided personal experience for my own children to feel the hospitality of others in many different settings.

Travel provides an opportunity for firsthand observation that can make a story or time in history come alive. Reading about the Civil War gave some insight into the terrible atrocities that occurred, but visiting battlegrounds and hearing the stories that took place on that land created pictures in our minds. Once we visited the Potomac area, and in our car on the way up, we listened to a rendering of George Washington's experience during the cold winter of the Revolutionary War. It happened to be a rainy, cold day on our visit. The hunger and shivering of the weary soldiers became more real in our imaginations as we looked out from car windows drenched by pouring rain.

Several summers, our children organized Mother's Days Out camps, and from these each earned their own money to pay for a portion of a planned history tour. From planning and hosting these creative camps for children in our backyard, they saved and saved. The airfare, food, and museum fees for the history tour were actually paid for by the teens.

Because missions in Communist Eastern Europe was a part of my own story, Clay and I planned for me to take each child, when they were fifteen or sixteen, on a mission journey with me to visit where I had worked. This gave us time to save our pennies toward the "high school mission trip with Mom." But it also provided me time alone with each child to speak into their lives, to undergird them with personal time, to imagine with them what they might want to do to invest their lives to bring light and beauty to their world as they emerged from our home into the world. This plan ended up being a gift at a crucial time in each of their lives. I could not have afforded to take our whole family on a trip to Europe, but one-on-one was much more fruitful. Besides, having six of us together would have meant much distraction and caring for others. Having focused time alone was significant for our relationships and for creating a sense of vision and value for life. It was sort of a graduation gift that all anticipated.

I have been so grateful that, through the years, Clay has supported my love of missions by allowing me to experience this with each child. Every family has a unique story or independent desires for a legacy they might want to pass on, and each legacy is worthy—all the more if it is important to you. Your life does not need to look like our lives, but you can use your imagination about what particular ways you would like to develop your own traditions, celebrations, and values for the shaping of your family culture.

Within a hundred miles of every town I have lived in, there are museums, historical homes, battlefields, places of interest that will bring much pleasure, imagination, and cultural experience to enhance the wonder of your children as they interact emotionally with the stories and expressions of the people and places they visit. Perhaps visiting a relative might open doors to new and interesting places.

Historical trips

Many have heard of "the Clarksons' historical journeys." My friend and I would plan a several-thousand-mile trip together. (Both of our husbands had weeks of 24/7 work in the spring, so that was a good time for us to adventure together.) We would search out historical places, fun or interesting museums, nature centers, and even famous restaurants along the way. Piling our seven children plus us into a Suburban, we charted out where we would stay, how far we would get in a day, and what we would visit.

Often, we would take snacks such as fruit, lunch meat, nuts, cheese, bread, or crackers and picnic at rest stops along the way to save money. It gave our children a place to run and eat before getting back in the car. At every stop, the older kids in the back seats would rotate to the next seat to their right, so that everyone had to sit in the back and middle—and so there could be no complaining about us being unfair. Joy sat in the middle of the front seat as a toddler and preschooler.

If we were going on a trip to Washington, DC, we would pick books on tape or stories pertaining to what we would be seeing (George Washington's home, the National Gallery of Art), and we would look ahead of time at some of the artists and subjects in the Smithsonian science and history museums. Then when we visited the places, they would already be familiar.

Theater, musicals, movies, and drama

Plays, musicals, theater, and drama left a deep impression on all of us. The first time we saw the theatrical production of *Les Misérables* in Colorado Springs, we were all transfixed by the dramatic story. The music was superb, and the story captured our hearts. Never was the mercy, kindness, and forgiveness of God more real than seen through the eyes of the priest who forgave Jean Valjean. (You'll have to experience it yourself—I don't want to give too much away.)

Many of our favorite plays were watched as movies: *West Side Story* with its theme of prejudice, *Romeo and Juliet* as a follow-up (gangs, bias, and violence that exudes out of such prejudice). The Jane Austen movies and books gave us a peek into the life and times of England when women had no inheritance rights.

We collected movies that were engaging and adventurous, with heroes, history, and humor—films that were family friendly (especially when all were young). Great movies are stories that become personified graphically in our minds. How important it is to seek the best quality of script, filming, acting, and story line. Saturday nights were group movie nights with friends or just with family to enjoy a great story. (I did have many nights when I entertained Joy in her room, because the content that was okay for teens was not appropriate for an immature, innocent young mind.)

Movies and plays gave us great opportunity to invite friends and to have rousing discussions about themes in life and issues we wanted them to wonder about. These are the experiences that captivated Nathan's wonder-filled ideas as he eventually became a story maker through his movies and scripts and his profession as an actor and writer.

Museums, conferences, concerts

Each year we purchased passes to museums in whatever area where we were living—art, science, historical, cultural, and botanical as well as nature centers and more. Clay often took the kids on Saturday mornings to the places near our home so that I could write!

Because we had yearly passes, we would tour the exhibitions and paint or draw what we saw, or walk through the exhibits, usually only until everyone was restless. I didn't want them to dread going to museums, and so we learned a little at a time and let what we had been exposed to sink in through discussion. But over many years, even if the ventures were short, the visits and exposure built a legacy of appreciation of the arts.

Clay found conferences or camps to take the boys to: Christian Magician Conference for Nathan, since he did birthday parties for kids; Singer-Songwriter Weekends for both boys as they were both interested; photography days; computer courses; and chess clubs. All of this was over a lifetime, not all at once. And so their exposure to many areas built a file drawer in their brain to be aware of many different subjects.

Book clubs, "Inking" gatherings, arts teas hosted by a friend each season, local dramatic productions and concerts (outdoors and indoors), weekend and weeks-long seminars, tennis, volunteer positions (library reading time), a special manners class that ended in a formal banquet for all of their friends (by a creative mama who made a business from it!) were ways the girls (and sometimes our boys) also found engagement.

Lessons, Events, Experiences

As our children grew from the young years to young adults, we would add more experiences, lessons, and activities that expanded their own personal engagement in life and the arts. Basic knowledge was gained through research papers that were on topics of interest to each one.

Activities or clubs, such as speech and debate, chess, photography, drama, gardening, and a French cooking class, were outlets to expand on interesting opportunities as they became older. These commitments also allowed for a wider community of friends and companions. All of our children were involved in an amphitheater professional production for six months out of the year, on weekends, for three years in Texas. With 150 people acting, singing, and engaging together on stage, including Clay and me, all grew into the appreciation and understanding of performance, personal discipline while on stage, costumes, makeup, and integrity of performance. It just happened to be something near our little country home for a few seasons.

Other years included performance choirs, tennis teams, being a junior docent for two summers at a historical house (including period dress), music lessons, summer conferences, world view weeks, arts teas, play performances, speech and debate, working at craft fairs, taking art lessons, participating in seasonal home decoration, hosting parties, and dress-up events; all were a part of our lives over the years.

I am limited by time and space in covering all the ways our family enjoyed life in cultural activities, and remember, they were spread out over many years, but these influences had a huge impact on our children's imaginations, on their wondering about life callings, and in shaping messages.

Amazing to me is that it was this area that captured the imagination of each child when they developed their career choices. Sarah became a creative writer and won an international writing competition in Oxford three years running. Joel, a composer, conductor, musician, creative voice-over artist, and author is doing research in theology and is working in choral music, theology, and the arts. Nathan became a professional actor, scriptwriter, movie producer, and author and continues to write imaginative books and movie scripts. Joy is teaching courses and loves to pass on inspiration to college students through the ideas of theology, imagination, and the arts. She hosts a popular podcast, *Speaking with Joy*, that explores the arts and imagination with contemporary as well as classical artists, musicians, and writers.

Each family will have their own backgrounds, passions, values to pass on to their children. You might be a family of medical experts, scientists or engineers, teachers, farmers, politicians, craftsmen, cooks, or gardeners. Impact often comes through the cultural background in which we were born and the cultural activities of our lives. But a vast exposure to cultural values, arenas, and messages is such a foundational part of our world today. Culture making deeply influences the trajectory of a generation as they express through these mediums what is of value. Cultural engagement is essential to a well-rounded education about the world and life.

You can use your imagination
about what particular ways
you would like to develop
your own traditions,
celebrations, and values
for the shaping of
your family culture.

10

The Battle and Joy of Shaping a Wonder-Filled Home

Generally, by the time you are Real, most of your hair has been loved off, and your eyes drop out and you get loose in the joints and very shabby. But these things don't matter at all, because once you are Real, you can't be ugly, except to people who don't understand.

Margery Williams, *The Velveteen Rabbit*

Therefore, do not throw away your confidence, which has a great reward. For you have need of endurance, so that when you have done the will of God, you may receive what was promised.

Hebrews 10:35–36

Home: The Laboratory of a Wonder-Filled Life

Mama, I have been thinking a lot about our home. I didn't know any other kind of a home. Now I see that I took for granted that not everyone grew up in a place of comfort where they felt invited to explore life, to eat great food, to read, create, have a community of like-minded people, to breathe in the visual and soul reality of faith. And now, I am beginning to realize how much time and effort it cost you. I just want to say thank you for being willing to invest by faith in something that we now see as wonderful.

This from a child who had forayed out into the world and found that lifegiving home building required a lot.

Eventually, I received a similar letter from all of my children, which was quite gratifying. However, there were so many years when I wondered if my ideals were actually moving us forward, if I would make it through the piles of housework or die first, and if my kids would ever appreciate what they had amid the swirl and demands of life. Yet now I know that my will to persevere in ideals, and to move forward one day at a time, had created a legacy.

Many have asked me if I would change anything about our journey together. The only thing I would change would be to demand that everyone who has their children at home have a full-time housekeeper.

I know that Michelangelo was said to have come down from the scaffolding of his masterpiece painting in the Sistine Chapel dirty, dusty, and rumpled from head to toe every day. And yet the remaining beauty of his creation is unprecedented. So it is with the building of a home culture.

In our book, *The Lifegiving Home*, my daughter Sarah expressed, as an adult, how she evaluated our home.

But my parents understood that the world that they made within the walls of our house was what constituted home. So I grew up in spaces framed by art and color, filled with candlelight, marked by beauty. I grew up within a rhythm of time made sacred by family devotions in the morning and long conversations in the evening. I grew up with the sense of our daily life as a feast and delight; a soup-and-bread dinner by the fire, Celtic music lilting in the shadows, and the laughter of my siblings gave me a sense of the blessedness of love, of God's life made tangible in the food and touch and air of our home.

It was a fight for my parents, I know. Every day was a battle to bring order to mess, peace to stressful situations, beauty to the chaos wrought by four young children. But that's the reality of incarnation as it invades a fallen world. . . .

What my parents—bless them—knew . . . is that to make a home right in the midst of the fallen world is to craft out a space of human flesh and existence in which eternity rises up in time, in which the Kingdom comes, in which we may taste and see the goodness of God.[1]

There is great value to building a secure and beautiful home life for everyone who dwells there. Home gives deep roots and a heritage of profound faith and provides a place of innocence, where gradually one may grow strong. Home provides a place of belonging in an isolationist world. Home gives us a people to belong to in a committed community of unconditional love. Home provides a place to celebrate and uphold godly character, righteous choices, living faith undistracted by the daily draws of the world. Home is a shelter in the midst of life's storms. Home is a lighthouse to others who are lost in the storms of life. The keeping of home shapes people forever.

> *Home gives us a people to belong to in a committed community of unconditional love. . . . The keeping of home shapes people forever.*

Creating the World of Your Home

We each live in worlds of our own making. The place we shape and create to live in says a lot about our own souls, our own vision for life. Perhaps my story can give you ideas you might build upon. Creating a world that breathed life within the walls of our home was what constituted home in our collective imaginations through many years and countless seasons together.

Home building takes many years and lots of effort to arrange life, with spaces framed by art and color, filled with inspiration and comfort, marked by aesthetic pleasure.

Give yourself time over many years to build your home well. Littles can make life overwhelming at first. Stretch in your capacity to be patient, to gently train your children to grow into maturity and self-control, and to understand that your consistent effort will, in time, produce fruit in their lives. The preschool and kindergarten years are the times you *start shaping appetites*, creating the life that will become expected reality. You are free to use your own desires and personal preference in creating life there. And just breathe in peace and rest as often as possible. I promise these years matter and they do pass, slowly by days, quickly by years.

Every day in each inch of space, each rhythm of time, each practice of love, we have the chance to join God in coming home, in living so that we make a home of this broken and beautiful world all over again. Love is enfleshed in the meals we make, the rooms we fill, the spaces in which we live and breathe and have our being.

We planted seeds of faith and a love for theology. Creating a daily life as a feast and delight in knowing, growing, and learning to serve by practice in serving shaped character. The laughter over my children's antics gave, as Sarah said, "a sense of the blessedness of love, of God's life made tangible in the food and touch and air of our home." We must value this "mess" of life and exhibit joy within for children to feel it is indeed a joyful place to dwell.

Melodies of a well-orchestrated life played through the rooms and cozy places throughout our home. On any given day, if you could peek inside my house, you would find life brimming over with color, sounds, tastes, rousing conversations, laughter, sometimes bickering, engagement in every inch of the space shared there.

Books would be strewn through all the rooms, some left open; art and nature paintings and prints standing tall on easels; framed family photos of grand memories made together strewn here and there as reminders of our clan and the loyalty and love we cultivated and expected. Resources for play (games, dress-up clothes, blankets and closets for tents); resources for creating art, such as colored pencils, paints, an easel filled with children's masterpieces, paper for drawing, sticker books; play dough and Legos for constructing while listening to music or a book on tape; and bubbles and sidewalk chalk for outdoor engagement, as well as swords, sticks, stones, and sand. The baby and toddler years found our home stocked with shape sorters, puzzles, board books, musical toys, and all sorts of colorful artifacts and soft stuffed animals to pretend with, as well as countless soft blankies to grab at any moment.

Thumping out strains of a song on my old, slightly-out-of-tune childhood piano, a child would be humming the familiar tune as he attempted to play by ear the melody of a musical score another child had used minutes before. A Lego city was added to while the beloved golden retriever slept happily close by. Watercolors, prints, small pieces of original art, elaborately illuminated and gold-framed verses all covered walls in every room. Baskets of books and magazines adorned every bedroom. Giggles, noise, and small messes ebbed and flowed through all the moments. Toy cars zoomed over imaginary roads. Soldiers, knights, princesses were seen running through rooms and hoisting flags on outdoor forts.

Wild games of capture the flag, *Roxaboxen* towns, water and piles of dirt, and outdoor tents sequestering pirates, explorers, and inventors lived in our various yards. Though peeking into a moment of our lives might give the impression of a haphazard or random lifestyle, this impression would be wrong. Clay and I were very intentional about how we set up our home and the practices and rhythms that took place every day. (For more inspiration, please refer to my books *The Lifegiving Home* and *The Lifegiving Table*.)

Soul Satisfaction of Participating in Life Together

I never knew how deeply fulfilling and satisfying this life of sharing together every day would be to me as I was tending it. I remember one day thinking in great surprise, *Being a close family community is so deeply satisfying.* This because I had never experienced such intimate closeness as a child.

And this after a number of years of working at it. Now that my children are adults, they are truly my best and most intimate, trusted friends. Our little community of Clarksons, with all of our peculiarities, limitations, and challenges, is our mutual favorite place of being and gathering. We all long to be together and relish holidays as the high points of our year.

We share in common our ideas, ideals, books, philosophy, world view, favorite Scripture. We like the same brand of tea. We talk a lot when together. Asking our children for their opinions about what we were writing or speaking shaped them as well as our messages. It took so much time to live a lifetime of engaging them in our own work, but writing and speaking was a natural fruit of their lives because we regularly planted so many seeds of communicating that they lived into year by year.

And so it is with other aspects of life. Cooking, organizing, cleaning, gardening, building, music, art, hospitality, ministry are caught by children when taught and practiced as a common occurrence.

Scripture tells us to "do all to the glory of God" (1 Corinthians 10:31). Though I was flawed, I did *give* my all to be excellent, to be generous in lifegiving hospitality, to seek to inspire through my words and devotions, to love with all of my heart, giving enthusiasm and spirit to this wonder-filled life.

Different seasons of life found different activities and toys, according to the children's needs at various ages. And, yes, a full life meant there were more messes to steward, more work to be done. But a lifegiving home did indeed nurture a life of wonder, exploration, and discovery.

In the long run, I found it to be a worthy commitment. David danced before the Lord with all of his might, and I have often had that thought in my mind of wanting to dance before God with all of my might as I filled my home with His reality through many dimensions (see 2 Samuel 6:14).

Were there conflict, challenge, weariness, discouragement at times? Yes, of course. I was a warrior fighting to bring light into a dark world. I had few support systems and fewer encouragers who believed in what I was doing. Yet one more quiet time, one more reflection on our ideals, and it would take me through another day, another year. And truly, the seed was growing deep roots that eventually manifested fruit.

Keeping God at the Center

Jesus took His disciples with Him everywhere. So we did as well; passing on values, truth, vision, morals happens in big and small moments, as we are walking through life. Deuteronomy reminds us of the necessity of keeping a 24/7 mindset in shaping the hearts of our children.

Instructing the Israelites about how important it was to teach their children about himself, God said,

> "You shall love the Lord your God with all your heart and with all your soul and with all your might. These words, which I am commanding you today, shall be on your heart. You shall teach them diligently to your sons and shall talk of them when you sit in your house and when you walk by the way and when you lie down and when you rise up. You shall bind them as a sign on your hand and they shall be as frontals on your forehead. You shall write them on the doorposts of your house and on your gates."
>
> Deuteronomy 6:5–9

Following this pattern, we sought diligently to follow and teach His wise ways morning, noon, and bedtime as we walked through life.

First the Bible, then an array of stories read aloud, marked rhythms of each morning as we all sat together.

Setting the Life Routines in Motion

Values and personality also entered into the shaping of our home. Clay and I are both musical. I have sung all of my life in different venues. Clay has been a singer-songwriter from the beginning of our relationship. We even recorded two albums together. Always, every variety of music, from classical to Celtic, accompanied all the moments, quietly in the background, and shaped our mutual tastes on varieties of songs and instruments.

What defines you and your family? Your answer will be different from ours. But you have the freedom to create a home life that suits your family and that cooperates with your personality and skills. Decide to embrace who you are and don't try to be someone else. Just commit, work, grow, and trust.

> *You have the freedom to create a home life that suits your family and that cooperates with your personality and skills. Decide to embrace who you are and don't try to be someone else.*

The outdoors is my own heart's delight. And walking miles every day is my beloved habit. My children have literally walked thousands of miles with me through mountain trails, city streets on trips, neighborhood areas. It is just a part of who I am, and so they learned to love it as well. *And* we had such fun—conversations, racing, chasing, enjoying being outside, which tends to neutralize bad moods. Hikes, walks, vigorous games of capture the flag or king of the mountain were energetically enjoyed. Candlelit dinners, from elaborate holiday fare to simple daily snacks, accompanied the familiar and beloved table times shared each evening and as all the interesting people came through our doors.

Each family is uniquely skilled and can create their own family culture—gardening, fixing cars, farming or raising animals, graphic design or art, cycling, medical care—so many legacies of heritage and preferences can become a part of a family culture. This is a place for each parent or teacher to pass on a part of their unique selves.

Next was play. Play establishes the truth of ideas heard and imagined deeply into the mind of a child. What she pretends becomes truth to the inner conscience. Play and pretend are faculties of our brain that allow us to perceive life beyond the boundaries of our normal life. We can believe in the bigger world because we have heard about it, pretended it, and imagined it. Play is serious work to the developing intellect of a child. Giving the mind a rest from constant input allows the brain to synthesize what it has been chewing on.

Play swords, a box of dress-up clothes from the thrift store (army pants, capes, elegant dresses, boots, jackets, hats) engendered pretend. Baking together, decorating for seasons together, having dreaming sessions—"If you could be anything when you grow up, what would you be?" "If you could travel anywhere, where would you go and who would you take?"— these sort of imaginings happened as we hiked, played, worked.

Some days we threw caution to the wind, grabbing jackets, crafting a quick picnic of whatever we could find easily, and piling into the car to release the wiggles and the wrinkles out of our relationships. We desperately longed for vacation days to *accomplish* nothing at all. Foraying into our wonderful world for a break, time to breathe, time to sally forth in rest, discovery, and pleasure was fairly common.

Wonder-Full Resources

Our home itself was a classroom of sorts. Interesting and compelling artifacts were placed in all the spaces of life. Much of what was learned was because there were bodies of knowledge (books, magazines, CDs, videos, puzzles) and ideas to explore at leisure in all corners of the house, without input from Clay or me. In general, a laboratory for life meant we had objects of interest in all the corners of our home, but we also intentionally limited technology except for certain times of the day. (The older our children became, the more privilege and responsibility they bore with technology.) Our home was cluttered with beauty and endless objects of interest.

As Sarah remembers, "Photographs plastered walls and sat on shelves to remind us of many momentous occasions. We did not have the luxury of a long-term 'family home,' but the heart of home followed us wherever we went."

And Joy wrote of home on her website,

When I peer back in my memory of childhood, I see books perched on every flat surface, I hear a favourite collection of instrumental Celtic songs singing out of a hidden CD player, I feel the vivid tesserae of a small mosaic of a hillside. . . . Over the hum of never ending argument and laughter of my siblings, I hear the kettle on the boil, and someone plucking out a Les Mis melody on our well beloved and out of tune piano. Beauty was more than mere decoration or entertainment in our home (though it was that as well), it gestured to, honoured, and expressed things we could not otherwise access. In a childhood marked by transience (we moved nineteen times), all these beautiful things seemed to capture and transmit some more permanent loveliness. So, my soul was wall papered with stories and songs and mountain vistas, and it all seemed very important.

One of my first and most stubborn convictions was that, despite itself, **the world is full of beauty,** that **our experiences of beauty are important,** and that, wherever we find it, **beauty gestures to something beyond itself.**[2]

Recognizing the Battle: A Whole Lot of Work for a Very Long Time

Dear Sally,

Every day, I hold ideals in my heart of what I want to create in my home, the way I want the learning in our home to be interesting, captivating, the ways I want to discuss great things at our dinner table. Then real life hits. My kids fuss, I become impatient, the house is constantly moving toward disorder, and I want to just throw in the towel. Is it really possible to create what you write about? Sometimes the mundane tasks overwhelm me and take over my vision. Am I the only one who feels this way? Am I a failure? Do I have the capacity to do what I can imagine but can't seem to live?

I often receive letters like this and meet with so many women who feel the same way. To build a civilized home life is the work of a lifetime, not achieved in a short period of time or without great effort and perseverance.

Recently I was at a gathering of women that reminded me of the reality of holding ideals and what it cost me over many years. Most present at the conference felt as though they were missing out by not being in the work world "to accomplish something tangible." Parenting and mentoring children is a very challenging life work. It costs your time, patience, and sacrifice over and over again for years on end. Like the Skin Horse in *The Velveteen Rabbit* said, when it is over,

> "most of your hair has been loved off, and your eyes drop out and you get loose in the joints and very shabby. But these things don't matter at all, because once you are Real, you can't be ugly, except to people who don't understand."[3]

Luckily, not *all* of my hair has been rubbed off yet! When we have been raised on voices that tell us women have the capacity to accomplish great feats, that they are intellectually capable of great thoughts and teaching, and that they have endless careers available to them, we can look at the whirlwind of messes and demands in our homes and wonder if we are accomplishing anything of value. Some moms have said to me, "I have my college degree and feel guilty that I am not using it or working a *real* job."

We live in a time that devalues the essence of hard work and perseverance. Looking for formulas to just make life easier, for instant order and success, is a search for many. I was never actually trained to work as hard as my life required me to, so it was quite a learning curve. But if we look at any great task, we understand that great results or accomplishments in life require long, enduring, and arduous work.

I am so grateful for heart surgeons, because I may need one someday to save my life. I will be more grateful for the amount of schooling, studying, bill paying, and endurance it cost him or her to become specialized in order to do surgery for my own benefit. Same with orchestra conductors, professors, writers, factory workers, store vendors who have added to my life because of their steadfast, faithful work.

All meaningful accomplishments in life require grit, hard work, time, vision, and commitment. Yes, my life involved more hard work and required more patience than I could have ever imagined at the beginning.

But we need to envision our lives as inspirers as a *great* work, worthy of our investment, to keep us moving ever forward. And we can have hope that our diligent work will nurture great souls, worthy of our investment.

One of the main reasons women feel discouraged is that culture does not generally affirm them in their role as moms. Demeaning the role of motherhood in general as a less valuable investment in life, experiencing a sense of "wasting my time" by giving themselves to their children, and suffering surely-someone-else-could-do-a-better-job syndrome are common temptations for women. As we look at the demands of and various messes inherent in our role, these messages can certainly discourage us. Yet, keeping our eyes on our ideals and goals will keep us moving forward.

Investment of Your Life Builds a Noble Legacy

As one who endured and persevered through the ups and downs of my journey to create a learning world of wonder, I want to come alongside you and say that *your life's work of seeking to be a mentor to your children, seeking to pass on a spiritual formation that creates a live faith, giving the training required to develop godly character, and creating a love for learning is absolutely one of the most profound works of our whole society and world.*

If you take the time to mentor your children, love them well, speak into their lives, give them a spiritually rich atmosphere, they will indeed surprise you. My children have all grown far beyond my expectations. That resulted out of their own personal direction and choice. But I learned more clearly that children are the most valuable resource of any country in all of history, and their capacity to excel, to create, to accomplish is vast because they were endowed with amazing capacity in their hearts, souls, and minds.

How they are shaped determines what they will become and to some degree what our own history will become. Little human beings require attention, nurture, love, and focused time in order to develop their capacity to become those who are strong, emotionally healthy, intellectually astute, and vibrant of spirit. To cultivate a great soul with excellent character is noble, good, right.

A garden has become a sort of metaphor for me in imagining the reality of my children's hearts, minds, bodies, souls. We would never suppose that if we threw good seeds into the wind they would suddenly become a flourishing garden. Similarly, if we threw the seeds of our children's lives and potential into the winds of a secular culture or storms of a worldly, materialistic life, hoping for them to flourish and land well, we could not expect them to become a well-planted and nourished garden. They would be subject to the arbitrary winds, storms, and predators of life.

God entrusted our children into *our* hands as one of the best works for which we answer to Him. He gave us the stewardship of shaping, investing in, and inspiring for His glory these little human beings entrusted into our hands by His love and design.

> *God entrusted our children into our hands as one of the best works for which we answer to Him.*

Because I had committed my whole life to Christ, one way for me to worship God was to serve these precious human beings He entrusted into my hands. God ordained family and home to have eternal value as the place our children are shaped in the transcendent image of God, through our homes. This is our most lasting legacy. Even as Jesus served us through His sacrificial life, so we model His love through our sacrificial life.

As human beings, children need nurture, attention, love, and training in order to access their potential. If neglected, they will grow only according to the personal nurture they have received. They are not just a commodity to be controlled, or beings to be organized into groups. Each is an individual of God's own crafting, with limitless capacity. And we must understand that God made all babies to be dependent, fragile, responsive to the care and love given them.

One thing I wish I had known and comprehended was how very long this journey of teaching four children to adulthood would be. It is a marathon, not a sprint. And of course, I was not trained for it, and as a pioneer in the home education movement, I was treading every step, every day by faith.

There are essential basics I wish I had known in order to avoid some of the unnecessary stress.

1. **Realistically counting the cost:** I wish I had had a realistic view of what it would cost me. Having never been trained and not having a model to follow from someone else's life made it challenging for me when I was exhausted. We did not have the support systems of family to help. As with any job, the work of passing on a love for learning can be arduous, long, and sometimes tedious. Since it is a marathon, pacing and planning a regulated and resilient life is best.

   Consequently, seek to evaluate and understand the scope of such a choice. We often tell our children, "When you get a shot, it will sting for just a little bit, and it might hurt for a little while afterwards, but you will be fine." If I had known ahead of time that passing on an inspired mind would "sting a bit" and require hard work, patience, and perseverance all along the way, I would not have struggled every time I experienced discouragement or frustration. I would have known that this was to be expected, understanding that these feelings are normal in any long-term endeavor, especially when dealing with immature children straining toward maturity. I would have understood that to be a normal part of the journey. I would not have worried so much along the way.

   Remember, for a parent to wrap her arms of love, elegance, character, and faith around the lives of her children to guide them, inspire them, nurturing the gift of wonder in their hearts, is a gift of inestimable value.

2. **Self-care and self-restoration:** Because it is a long journey to travel through the years with children, and because we are being depleted every day, all the time, we all need to set into place a daily restoration for ourselves.

   I had to learn that there was no one, not even my husband, who could recognize my depletion, my weariness along the way. So, years into this, I had to begin to set aside focused time alone; time with friends to just play and escape the burdens of life, times to read and be re-inspired. Because we are always giving out, we must also always be in the process of filling up. This will be a little different for each person. Honoring your personality and particular desires and needs will restore you a little each day. If you spend all of your emotional or physical coins, so to speak, you will have to add back to the bank of yourself in order to have more to spend.

3. **Taking time for recreation:** We have bodies, hearts, minds, and we need rest, pleasure, friends, love, and recreation in order to best thrive. Because we have seventeen years or more to shape each child, we do not need to be frenetic about getting everything accomplished in a year or two. Between all the children, I had someone at home that I was educating for twenty-eight years. It meant I had to shake it up and give grace to our days along the way.

    Taking breaks and enjoying local amusements (seasonal fairs, holiday celebrations, museum exhibits, travel, time to play, hospitality to invite people into our world, time for hobbies) means that we will not feel that we have left all of life behind, but that our holistic way of life is sustainable and regenerative.

    Refer to the culture chapter (chapter 9); we took lots of time to explore and go to interesting places, and it gave dimension and space to have fun and relax.

4. **Recognizing your limitations, your children's limitations:** Accept yourself for who you are. You will be better at some subjects than others because you are a human being with a God-given personality. No amount of work or performance according to someone else's standards will ever make you a perfect teacher. Your children will have strengths and weaknesses, not of your own making, but because of personality, age, ability, calling, and the life circumstances of you and your children. Your personal story is the place where you need to live confidently.

Don't compare yourself to others. Your home, your children, your story will be unique and better served if you decide to embrace them and like them. You will become disgruntled at times, impatient, exhausted, overwhelmed. But in reality, all parents of all children feel this way. When you find danger signals and can see fear, self-criticism, or a sense of failure, make a plan for how to restore you, the mentor.

Go to conferences or retreats that build you up. Plan a one-woman outing for coffee or time with friends each week, if possible. Start a small-group Bible study or book club in your home and build friends with the same values because of what you are reading together. Clay took our children out on Saturday mornings, and it was a reprieve for me. You are human, and you will make some mistakes. Live in the grace and acceptance of a humble, gentle, merciful, compassionate Father.

5. **Keeping housework from overwhelming:** We each have a breaking point. My kids said that almost every time they remember me "blowing," exploding in frustration or anger, I was at the sink with dirty dishes. Having children in the house all the time means there will be messes all the time. Keep making plans for how to simplify the areas that are most challenging for you and engage your family in the work.

Throw out junk, piles, papers, mail on a regular basis. When it builds up, take a day, with everyone helping, and get things back in order. Sometimes we would take a week to clean out, throw out, bring order. I learned that messes and things being out of order were what would put me under.

I would rather eat beans every day and save to have someone come into my home to deep clean once in a while than to always feel like we were out of control or that I had to do it one more time. Do what you need, your way, and take time to bring order, at least once in a while. And as I said, my kids grew up knowing that they would always be a part of the workforce to continually keep bringing order.

6. **Grace for the stages:** Having lots of littles means you will be giving, not sleeping as much, spreading your energy on meeting the
   physical needs of your babies and toddlers all the time (nursing,
   changing diapers, holding, rocking, feeding, playing, cleaning up all
   the time, every day). I see the "little" years as a sort of boot camp
   of life. But in the midst of this season, talk to your children, read
   to them often, take them outdoors, kiss them often. Watch how
   they marvel at each leaf, at bugs that are sheer mysteries to their
   imagination—every day a miracle of great proportions to them.

   Don't feel like you need to give some kind of curriculum to your
   child too early unless they are interested. Just enjoy, offer lots to discover, and don't create unnecessary stress and pressure. You will become used to this—I promise. Your mom muscles will grow stronger
   with use. Believe by faith that this demanding season will pass and
   will not always be this hard—and that someday you will miss babies.
   Truly. Many try to buy curriculum and require too much work too
   early. When your child frustrates you by wiggling too much, you have
   probably required too much seat work. You have a whole lifetime
   ahead of you to dive into a more demanding schedule. Remember
   how important creative play and development are to their long-term
   well-being.

   Kindergarten to around age twelve are often the golden years when
   progress is much more evident. Read, explore, give chores and things
   to create and ponder and write. These are years, in general, for natural
   times at home to grow, learn, and strain toward understanding bigger
   and bigger concepts, and to gather knowledge.

   Middle school and high school years are times for patience, again.
   This time with moods that swing and sway in a moment's time. You
   are moving your child from immaturity to a place where they will
   have to use their own muscles in every area of life. Yet they are still
   hormonal, immature, lacking perspective and experience. Stick close
   to your teens; tell them how much you like them and try to mean
   it. They will soon be entering an adult world filled with challenges,

temptation, loneliness, work to master, and adult responsibility. These are the years we focused on mentoring, discipleship, talking late into the night about issues that were on their hearts. And I took each out to breakfast or coffee on occasions so that I could speak into their hearts alone with them, according to their needs. (Why do teens open up so much better at night?! And with food?)

Activities increase as children grow older—classes, sports, debate, acting, singing, jobs, community, and service become places of need as teens require more broad friendships. It is desirable for all people to have friends and companionship. You host many events at your home, get to know the companions of your teens, stay close and relational so that you are still welcomed into their secrets and decision-making processes. Don't just assume things will be okay, but be a servant leader during these times and invest personal interest even when they are a bit argumentative, because they are wrestling with the world and need your input, love, and support more than ever.

Remember, the teen years are the time you are beginning to launch and give wings to their own ideas and dreams. Trying to control teens often results in rebellion. Affirm and provide places for them to have some independence of opinion and taste. Hold fast to the ideals that are nonnegotiable. Be sure you have invested emotionally in believing forward in their lives so that they will be open when there are places where you feel a need to draw boundaries. Remember, be *for* them. Create an atmosphere of hospitality and welcome your children's friends regularly with fun so that your home will be considered one of the best and most accepting places to be.

So much more could be said, but make your home, always and forever, a place of welcome, refuge, fun, comfort, and delight. You will find the work inside its walls will hold influence for a lifetime. You will never stop "making home," because there will always be people in your world longing for the life that you have created there. But you will be remembered as the wise woman who built her house for eternity.

11

Securing Wonderful Rhythms, Routines, and Rituals

Ritual: A set of fixed actions sometimes performed regularly.

Routine: A fixed or usual way of doing things.

You will never change your life until you change something you do daily. The secret of your success is found in your daily routine.

> John Maxwell, *Success: One Day at a Time*

Take pains with these things; be absorbed in them, so that your progress will be evident to all.

> 1 Timothy 4:15

Those of us who have journeyed through the tales of Aslan might feel as though he could appear at any moment in our own pathways. I have a deep-seated thrill of emotion inside as I remember first hearing about Aslan breathing forth creation through song. It sparked an imagination of what actually took place at creation that continues to grow in my heart.

The CHRONICLES OF NARNIA books have spread their enchantment and sparked imagination for many years. English authors have cast many spells upon us as we have traveled the roads of their stories. I remember Tolkien weaving his magical tales of hobbits—normal, timid creatures like us, feasting and celebrating life. Suddenly, they are drawn away from their warm, comfortable homes to foray into a world of adventure, danger, sacrifice, friendship. Again the feeling of being there in the story bubbles up inside.

The Fellowship of Inspiration

Tolkien and Lewis were great friends. Their friendship kindled in each of them the creative energy to write the stories so enjoyed by readers all over the world. Tolkien actually helped Lewis come to faith. As close friends, they invested around twenty years meeting together each week in a pub to discuss one another's writing. I wondered if *The Fellowship of the Ring* was birthed from the legacy of their time together in the Eagle and Child pub where they met.

Lewis and Tolkien invited others to join them and learned to value this real-life, personal fellowship of creatives and writers. They deeply influenced one another just by celebrating this ritual for years on end that shaped their books, soul messages, and lives. Discussing their writing, building deep pathways of friendship, and living in the companionship of those alive with words and ideas formed the destiny of their own literary legacy. We can only imagine how their stories became more fascinating, exciting, and real because of the rhythms of commitment to meet in their local pub each week.

Diana Glyer, author and C. S. Lewis expert, writes about the Inklings, a community of writers who gathered in friendship and fellowship for almost two decades. She describes this auspicious group of friends:

> When half a dozen members had assembled, Warren Lewis would produce a pot of very strong tea, the men would sit down and light their pipes, and C. S. Lewis would call out, "Well, has nobody got anything to read us?" Someone always did. Out would come the rough draft of a story or a poem, and the others would settle down to listen, to encourage, to critique, to correct, to interrupt and argue and advise. They'd continue this way, reading aloud, energetically critiquing, until two or three in the morning. And meetings went on like this every week for nearly twenty years.[1]

Of this wily group of friends, Lewis wrote, "What I owe to them all is incalculable. . . . Is any pleasure on earth as great as a circle of Christian friends by a good fire?"[2]

The commitment of meeting weekly over decades shaped the people and especially the messages they created. From their example we understand how regular commitments can transform lives, engender fresh creativity. As I also reflected on the stories of Jesus with His disciples, Socrates and Plato, and so many more friends throughout history, it was clear that making regular commitments over time shapes and often influences destinies. Regular relationships gathered around meaningful activity produce great souls. Consequently, determining the routine commitments that added value to our lives became a focused plan for us in leading our family.

Immeasurable Value of Repetition and Habits of Life

Even as Tolkien and Lewis found that their writing and lives were inextricably woven into each other's stories, so the history of a family is woven together over years of habitual ritual and routine shared. This chapter may seem repetitive to you if you read the chapter about pursuing treasures of knowledge. This chapter looks at the subject from a different point of view—how we fit all of these commitments into a schedule. So, hopefully, this will underline *the way to carry out our educational ideals in real time.*

That which we practice and participate in over and over again daily determines who and what we become. Clay and I realized early on the value of putting rhythms and routines in our lives to determine what we wanted one another and our family to become.

> *That which we practice and participate in over and over again daily determines who and what we become.*

With four demanding little human beings who wanted to be fed, played with, clothed, and provided for on a regular basis, we knew the life of constant interruption. Add to that responsibilities, duty to family and friends, keeping a home, ministry—let alone home education and writing books—we knew that unless we seized our days, they would just fly away into the oblivion of life demands.

We knew we needed some kind of routine to give order and stability to our ideals. What we practiced every day, all the time, as a routine and expected exercise established deeply held values that shaped our family culture, our sense of "We are the Clarksons. This is what we do, this is what we value, this is how we live."

Clay and I agree that most of our educational influence came from how we scheduled life and gave it a shape through our rhythms, routines, and rituals. What we practiced every day as a way of life probably influenced our children and their ultimate life messages more than the resources we provided. A home filled with meaningful rhythms gives foundation to life messages and values.

Establishing Rhythms

I pictured our rhythms of life as anchors in our days, those things that held us fast, that were our moorings to keep us from drifting in the winds of life. A rhythm in a song frames the recurrent beat that keeps the music moving forward systematically.

Because of our appreciation of the Inklings and the way Christ influenced His disciples and others, we determined that we would create structures that included a sort of co-mentoring by establishing rhythms of being together in everyday life. Commitment to a shared fellowship of learning community was a starting point.

Even as there are many instruments in the percussion section of an orchestra that give the beat and tempo of the forward progression of the music being performed, we had differing rhythm instruments that gave our lives stability and determined our own forward motion day by day. I will describe some of our rhythms that held us fast. And when everyone in the community cooperates with these rhythms, a sort of conformity to expectations falls into place.

Morning devotions

As I mentioned in a previous chapter, I practiced having time to read my Bible, to pray, and to center my life each day. *It was a necessity for me to keep perspective and fresh vision.* As an introvert, I craved time alone to gather my thoughts, to center my emotional needs, and to engage in the wisdom, truth, and beauty of relating to God. I also always had some book I was reading every day, even if only a few pages at a time. Some days were quite meaningful, some days I just sat and sipped my tea, but this was a foundation that held me through my days.

Of course some seasons made this more difficult. When I had little ones, I always had to adjust my schedule to make this happen. But even when my children were little, I needed this for my own well-being and peace of heart. When mamas give out every day, all the time, they must ensure that they are building rhythms that consider their own needs so that they do not become empty and overwhelmed. This deeply felt need to start my day this way was so important to me that I would arise early just to have a few minutes alone.

I would quietly get out of bed (not even Clay was welcomed into my personal quiet space), tiptoe to the kitchen, brew a cup of tea, light a candle, put on soft music, and sit in my big, overstuffed quiet-time chair. My children came to expect that this was "Mama's time" and learned to entertain themselves for a few minutes if they awakened while I was sitting in this chair.

Of course, I really could not have quality time when they were awake milling around the house until they were older and understood my need for utter aloneness. But I did spend many a morning up very early just to be sure I had this time. Countless times, it was during these quiet moments that I would garner ideas, plans, inspirations for my life and for our days. Quiet is needed to cultivate wonder and imagination.

Next, we had a simple breakfast, usually scrambled eggs and toast (everyone learned to make them), and ate together. Devotions always followed this time. Over years, we read from many different devotional books, often something I had been learning in my own time of reading, and always Scripture at the core. This was followed by prayer every morning.

There are thousands and thousands of days that children spend growing up in a home. Think of these important rhythms as building a place in the soul of your family, one brick, one day at a time. Cumulatively, thousands of days of practicing meeting with God at the beginning of the day create an expectation in each one as something we should always do for the rest of our lives. And so their spiritual lives were built into a strong fortress of truth one day, one brick at a time.

And so, in some shape or form, each of us still arises every day to spend time with the Lord. It is about us being able to come to Him, personally, as we are. We ponder His stories, His heart; we look for His fingerprints as we ask Him to guide our day. We tell Him we love Him day after day, and these sweet memories are imprinted on our minds and hearts forever. It became a mutually expected rhythm for every day for all of us.

Read-aloud time

Since a word-rich environment was the key to developing strong mental muscles, it was a priority in our schedule. Every day, the first practice of our home, after devotions, was to gather and read together for a half hour to an hour and a half. Again, laying bricks in the foundations of their mind palace, building a large edifice to hold thoughts, ideas, truth, virtue, and all the knowledge that would feed their thoughts.

Reading together provided context for strong friendships like the one Tolkien and Lewis shared. It documents every day that this value is important to our lives, and the habit of reading serves our brains, souls, and spirits for a lifetime. This practice of reading daily served to provide a habit for a lifetime for all four children.

After reading time, each child completed at least one math lesson individually in whatever book they were studying. (In math, we used age-graded curriculum, but we did not necessarily study it the year it was expected. They just completed one book and went to the next, with no artificial structures of time limits.) They completed a ten- to fifteen-minute individual language arts workbook lesson, and this brought us to late morning.

Play and pretend

Because our minds are created to grow, to know, and to access knowledge, brains love time to review, refresh, and even passively sit in the information just learned. But to be effective, brains need free space, free from flooding, so to speak; in order to receive information, there must be time to absorb what was given. This is why is it is so important to keep children from the constant entertainment of machines—their brains need free space to digest thoughts.

Brains love to have time to stretch into what they have exercised. Even as Pilates helps a body be healthy by stretching the muscles and bringing relaxation, play and pretend do the same thing for a brain. If the brain has been stimulated, then giving it "stretching time" to live into what it has just ingested helps the information become more deeply planted.

A child's play exercises her imagination and solidifies as truth what she has been learning. Romping all over our land gave rousing, stomping, yelling time to live deeply into the stories and adventures that were just read.

Play is serious business to both children and adults. Without recreation of some kind, we are more subject to manifesting stress in our bodies. Play, pretend, hiking a mountain trail, rocking in a chair on a front porch, playing hopscotch, resting, drinking a cup of tea or coffee and munching nuts, skipping rope, and dashing about with pretend swords against imaginary enemies are just a few examples of the therapy or stretching that can give the brain rest or recreation. Providing our thought muscles a passive place to synthesize and coordinate new knowledge with the knowledge previously stored creates roadways of communication in the brain.

Even as a body needs sleep to restore, the brain needs recreational time to ingest well the ideas engaged. Sometimes play can actually become what we might call work. Painting, playing an instrument, baking, or gardening can be work, but the mind loves to work in creative pursuits. Play and creativity are vital to the strength and well-being of a brain.

Physical exercise also promotes in the brain happy hormones that further strengthen thought patterns. In the same way a body can become exhausted from overstimulation, the brain can become fatigued by overexposure to hours of sitting still just trying to engage new data. Because the brain is always working, it requires visual and mental rest to stay efficient. It is the reason that sometimes after a long sleep, the answer to a difficult problem will surface because the brain has had time to work on it without overstimulation. So sleeping is also what is needed before an academic test, as the brain works on what it has taken in even when we are at rest.

Lunch was next. Did I mention our family loves to eat and drink?

Afternoon reading and quiet hour

I am repeating a pattern I wrote about earlier in the book as it neatly fits into this section of rhythms and routines—and was a profoundly important discipline that shaped our children's habits and brains!

Each afternoon, I established an hour of time in which each of us would go to our own space and spend the hour reading. I placed a basket of books in each child's room that included one of each of these:

fiction of my choice
fiction of their choice
biography

science or nature

history

fun, creative photograph book

When they were young, a basket of small rewards for every few books finished was a great lure. (Dollar store sorts of stuff: bubbles, sidewalk chalk, stickers, a sticker book, an activity book, a small toy, a puzzle, a car or truck, a coloring book, etc.) When they finished the agreed-upon number of books during their quiet hours and could narrate them back to me, they were able to pick whatever they wanted from the basket. This helped establish our quiet hour and gave them a reason to do it.

Over time, I found that this was such a normal expectation of what the Clarksons did every day that everyone, even my extroverts, loved having time alone—and they still do. What we practiced became an expectation, and they saw value in the discipline of an hour alone.

My children devoured hundreds of books during this time. It was one of the best rhythms we practiced. It led to self-learning and a love for knowledge and gave an education all its own. When I was a young mom, an older friend told me it was the best routine their family had ever established, and so I worked at it day after day and it has served all of us well. And it gave me a few minutes by myself in which I usually had my own one-woman tea time.

When our children were toddlers, they would take a nap during this time. But as they got older, I would set a timer for fifteen minutes and say, "This is your special time to play and look at picture books and listen to your music. When the timer beeps, you may come tell me about what you did!" Then I would add more time to the timer as they were able to manage, and eventually, especially when it was a practice for our whole family, the younger ones complied with what the older ones practiced. We usually set aside an hour.

Civilizing our day with tea time

A habit I picked up from living in Europe was a daily afternoon tea time. It sounds more formal than it was in our home. Whether in England with an afternoon tea or in Vienna with the *Kaffee und Kuchen* (coffee and cake), having lived in both countries for considerable time, I learned that taking a fifteen- to twenty-minute break together was quite civilized and enjoyable. Turning on our electric teakettle, putting out a snack, and sipping a strong cup of something enjoyable became our practice whenever anyone was home and always when the kids were small. I might have given them something refreshing besides tea, though they all started fairly young with this habit. (For littles, I would make their tea three-quarters milk with a couple teaspoons of tea to make it a little bit brown—and always out of a real mug or cup when they learned to be careful. I even do this now with Lilian, my two-year-old granddaughter.) The break always felt like a treat. Friendship evolved from cherished moments of pure rest and refreshment. To this day, all of us stop for tea every afternoon as a lifetime habit wherever we are in the world. I am quite sure the practice has probably saved our lives on many occasions.

> *Friendship evolved from cherished moments of pure rest and refreshment.*

Five o'clock cleanup

A memory of my mother rushing to straighten up our home stuck in my mind. After she had us race around with her, she would put on bright red lipstick and then make some kind of refreshing drink and nibble for when my father walked through the door a bit later. I remember asking her why she did this. Her reply stuck. "Your father is surrounded by women in his office every day who are beautiful and smart. I want to help him have a reason to come home, to be at ease, to find 'his' people waiting for him. It is a way of continuing to build our friendship." (My father highly respected my mother for her intellect, companionship, and partnership in life. Her habit of considering him in kind ways added time to their own relationship. It was not a nonfeminist behavior but a thoughtful extension of friendship, making room for honoring the relationship.)

Consequently, for my own sanity and to have an end to our day that moved in the direction of some order, I practiced my own end-of-the-day routine. It made me feel better on the demanding nights, but also gave order to our home for all of us, including Clay. (More on that later in this chapter.)

Dinnertime discipleship: the lifegiving table

The past years, my adult children have all agreed that one of the greatest pleasures is coming home to our dinner table to feast, talk, and be friends. Feasting came to mean our celebration of eating together, even if it was a bowl of oatmeal. I am quite sure they did not realize how much of a security and grace this was to develop close friendships, to establish that we were a community that belonged to one another. Yet it is the one thing everyone agrees on now, that our eating together was a gift to all.

It has been clearly established in numerous research studies that a family who eats together ends up being closer and shares mutual values for a lifetime. We need food, but it is also pleasurable for most people to eat and drink, to stop working, to enjoy a meal, and to share in companionship. (Refer to the section "Express, discuss, expand ideas" in chapter 7.)

Having as an expectation that every night we would sit at the dining table and eat and discuss life, ideas, a book, a movie, a sermon, or a political issue, etc. shaped our children to become proficient at writing and speaking. Every night was an exercise in sharpening their communication skills by talking Torah, so to speak. This was an outcome of our lives in the same way that Tolkien and Lewis became best friends. They and we couldn't have known how deep the roots would grow from this simple commitment.

Nighttime reading

For many years when our kids were little, we would read together for at least fifteen minutes at night as a way of emotionally preparing them for the approaching bedtime. Usually this was a time of fun or adventuresome books. Sometimes we would read a favorite or fun series of books like THE CHRONICLES OF NARNIA or LITTLE BRITCHES or some similar reading to settle everyone down. But this happened in some seasons and not in others.

Summer found us outdoors until late. Winter necessitated that we stay indoors because of the cold. The point is, we had expected daily rhythms that focused on building a love for words, ideas, and truth, even at bedtime.

Our practices were pretty simple and straightforward: devotions, read aloud, play, personal reading time, cleanup, baths, and then nightly discussion. These shaped a love for learning, a life of wonder and exploration every day. This was more profoundly influential than any classes or curriculum or particular books we read as a part of our educational goals. These were the practices that gave root to the tree of all of our lives.

Because of our verbally rich atmosphere, our children all built an internal self-actualization that they were stewards of thoughts and messages. Each is an eager communicator in their own sphere of influence today. Because the shaping of this value was organically formed in the rhythms of a daily intake and expressive environment, choosing to be communicators as professionals came naturally.

Goodnight bedtime blessing

Convictions grew in our hearts that closing each day by bringing peace and providing affirmation, affection, and love was important. A nighttime blessing of each child ended the day in the air of dependable, generous love. Closing our day by asking God for His continued presence and grace would tie a bow of completeness around the day. Relationship and unconditional love as an expectation was another profound anchor that we wanted to practice each day, mooring us to our values. This was the goal of the nightly blessing, and of course, there were kisses all around!

Once these precious ones had bathed, brushed teeth, and readied for bed, Clay and I, or just one of us, would sit at the bed of each child and converse for a few minutes about what their day had held, find out what was on their little hearts, and then pray with them. If I was nursing a baby, I would come after for my kiss. Our prayers were simple and usually included thanks for that child, a blessing of peace for their hearts and minds, and a verbalization of love and commitment to our wonderful Father for taking care of our needs.

Of course, this is a general look at our days, and the teen years took their own form, but we wanted our children to hear and feel the love and blessing of our hearts as we put each day to rest and we practiced it for thousands and thousands of days. Even last year, when I lived in Oxford with Joy, one of us would always visit the bedside of the other and keep our ritual of blessing and prayer.

It would be easy to idealize our family and suppose we kept to these rhythms without resistance, but all of us were selfish, sinful, immature, messy, just as all human beings are. So these deeply held values lived into our practices amid the normal noise and activity of life because we knew that what we practiced together we would become. And if we missed the routine for a while, we just began again because it was so familiar and an anchor to our days.

Though there might have been fusses or conflict during the day, we had a rule that all of us, including Clay and I, had to make peace with one another before going to bed. It didn't mean that all issues were solved, but just that we would agree to give grace to one another and bind ourselves to a commitment to love. Again, this rhythm of loving one another and living it out through the moments of our days gave an expectation that "the Clarksons are going to be loyal no matter what. We are family. We are called to cover one another's faults with grace and forgiveness."

It would be easy to idealize our family and suppose we kept to these rhythms without resistance, but all of us were selfish, sinful, immature, messy, just as all human beings are.

Were there times when I wondered if my children would ever stop being petty or would choose to get along? Of course, but if I look back into the recesses of our family life, I now understand that there was health being built and love laying a foundation for future relationships that would hold them fast in their adult lives. Rhythms practiced produce long-term fruit.

Routines That Shaped Order

A home where there are constantly people needs to have a structure that moves chaos toward order on a regular basis. We gave our children the mental image that since they were a part of the family who eats, wears clothes, and lives inside the walls of their home, we also wanted them to feel the responsibility of keeping that home at least somewhat together.

Chore charts were a bridge too far for me. Figuring out which day for which child added pressure to my already full brain. Consequently, my children just learned to expect that all of them would do chores. But we did have expectations to help the day go a little bit more efficiently.

Daily expectations

Part of my educational model meant shaping our children's self-image as capable and created with capacity, agency, and responsibility. Understanding the constant burden of work, paying bills, keeping a house, and all that comes along with life meant that they needed to practice working as a way of life to prepare them for the reality of the responsibility they would have when they were older.

I will not include all of the ways we attempted to build strength in their habits of work. But the point is that regularly embracing the idea that "I have a responsibility to care for and give back to this community called family" is a part of the education that will prepare them to become responsible adults.

I actually don't think it matters in what way children are trained to this idea, as there are so many ways and so many differing personalities. But more important is that there are practices *every day* that prepare them to expect to work and to be responsible when they are adults. Becoming proficient in taking initiative to be responsible in one small way leads to the understanding of how this works in other areas. In other words, washing and drying dishes every day is a habit that will prepare an adult to take care of his greater home, because the value of working at it has been learned through one small task.

Mealtimes

One of the older kids set the table at each meal, while one had the responsibility of emptying the dishwasher (smaller children always did the silverware). One child rinsed the dishes after every meal, and another put them in the dishwasher or dried the pots and pans and put them away. Someone cleared and swept the crumbs from the table as well as from under the table. This is basic stuff, and we were always moving in the direction of keeping things somewhat orderly on a daily basis.

Putting it all together again

Sometime around five or so in the afternoon, I put on loud, fun music and set the timer for fifteen minutes, and everyone would attempt to put the house back together. Legos had their own box or shelf, puzzles had their own ziplock bags, books on shelves, toys on the shelves or in a closet—everything had a place to go. This attempt to at least keep our living areas to a semblance of organization not only helped me not to be overwhelmed, but I think that the practice of doing it every day gave my children a sense of responsibility for daily cleaning up.

Then There Was More

Certain days held specific exceptions and celebrations among the daily rhythms. Friday night was company night, and Saturday night was pizza and movie night. Saturday included a special breakfast time or sugared cereal, which was not eaten the rest of the week. Sunday breakfast with pancakes or French toast was always a bribe to get them out of bed and ready to go to church. Sunday afternoon we celebrated a more formal tea time with something sweet and a strong pot of English tea. There is more, but you can find out about all of these traditions and others in *The Lifegiving Home*.

The point is, we established a familiar family culture from our own imagination of what was important to us. Our rhythms were based on the personality of those inside our walls. Our culture created very close ties among all of us Clarksons by establishing daily, weekly, yearly routines. We were unified and yet very individual in personality. But our home cherished each one and allowed the freedom to access life potential for each. Each family can find their own rhythms, rituals, and routines. But it was the celebration of life in these mundane but thoughtful ways that kept our home happy and growing.

12

Never-Ending Wonder
for Lifelong Learning

Anyone who stops learning is old, whether at twenty or
eighty. Anyone who keeps learning stays young.

Attributed to Henry Ford

Finally, brethren, whatever is true, whatever is hon-
orable, whatever is right, whatever is pure, whatever
is lovely, whatever is of good repute, if there is any
excellence and if anything worthy of praise, dwell on
these things.

Philippians 4:8

Walking down the cobbled lanes of Oxford on a golden afternoon filled my little-girl innocent heart once again with giddy excitement. I imagined that these irregular lanes, where students and professors were bustling about, were the places where C. S. Lewis and J.R.R. Tolkien had life-changing conversations.

An important, unassuming meeting was my destination. Walking through the University Parks in Oxford, England, is a gift that I enjoyed almost every afternoon at precisely four o'clock. Meandering along worn pathways surrounded by budding trees gave a sort of benediction to my days of work. I was invited into a reverie of quiet and peace at the end of busy, adrenaline-filled hours.

This deliciously vibrant day my pathway seemed a symphony of delight: The green grass and leaves were singing life, the azure sky and billowing clouds were providing a background of dramatic tones, the birds were chilling flutes, the swans gliding were a symphony of elegance, and the flowing stream bubbled a lullaby.

In my midsixties, perhaps my wonder is heightened from so much practice of wanting to enter into the moment, to see from inside the beauty, to appreciate the seasons, to notice the color and design. I don't want to miss any beauty that might come my way. Knowing I would not always live in Oxford, I tried to enter into the wonder of the moment and mentally photograph the scenes to revisit when I moved back to the States.

The best part of these days was that I would meet my daughter, Joy, who is currently working daily on her PhD in St. Andrews, Scotland. Because Oxford has a bigger research library in her field, she was able to live there for a year, sharing an apartment with me.

A small lake, alive with ducks and two fierce swans, lay at the back of the park. We had named one of the benches that viewed that lake as our own, and we sat there almost daily while settling the ills of the world.

As friends do, we rehearsed all the moments of our day. Often, I wanted to take notes on the profound things she was learning through her reading and study that I wanted to remember. I never had the opportunity to study at an international university, and my eager mind still is hungry to learn.

A life of wonder never ends. It provides possibilities of grace, excitement, delight to enjoy every day if it is embraced as a way of life. Learning is a never-ending grace if it is valued and embraced. Appetites to grow, to learn, to become, to know are shaped by the priorities we live out in real time.

Learning should not be measured by twelve years of school. A love for learning is ignited to burn for a lifetime.

My relationship with my children just got better and better over time because of a shared way of observing and experiencing our world. Joy and I created a very full life together out of what we had practiced over years. So each day when I met with her, I knew I would learn and be stimulated to read more, think more, immerse my mind in new ideas.

Learning should not be measured by twelve years of school. A love for learning is ignited to burn for a lifetime.

Engaging in expansive theological ideas; discussions about music and art; and chatting about what to eat for dinner, emails received, commitments made, ideals and ideas learned filled constant streams of conversation. It was a fine way to close the day and to mentally lay all the burdens to rest as we moved into a more relaxing evening—and to get our ten thousand steps!

I thank you for wading through my thoughts and convictions in this book so patiently. I hope it has been of help or encouragement in some way. As I come to an end, I want to synthesize what I have written.

As I was chatting about this book with Joy on our little bench that had become a classroom of sorts to our own souls every day, my mind began swimming with convictions. I knew I needed to write *this* book you are reading now. I wanted to write about *what is possible* to encourage those who are farther back on the road. In spite of my own limitations and inadequacies, pursuing a life I believed was most excellent ended up, in the long run, being even more gratifying and fulfilling than I expected.

I realized that afternoon how much I have come to count my adult children as my friends, but also as colleagues in pursuing truth, learning, ideas, imagination. They have become my own most profound mentors because of the process of their own learning and growing through the ideals we pursued. (Sorry I repeated this, but I really, really want you to know it is possible to end well and to continue to grow in relationship.) Because all had embraced their own vision for life and were foraying into idealistic fields of study, creativity, and influence unique to themselves, as I said, I wanted to write a book to other parents to say, "*This is possible.*"

As I mentally surveyed my years and processed my conversation with Joy about writing this book, I realized that one of the best legacies of my whole life was the experience of having been the teacher of my own children. So, here it is.

In a world rampant with secularism and philosophies that negate belief in God, life requires that those of us who live by our belief in God must be focused and intentional in passing on wisdom, reality, foundations, truth, and purpose to our children.

The world is in dire need of wisdom and essential messages that will shape culture into a place that flourishes. As believers, we understand that shaping a biblical worldview and helping to redeem a dark culture is the responsibility of every one of us who follows Christ.

And those who say they are Christ followers should be the most excellent in character, civilized, gracious, winsome in behavior, and bringing light, goodness, and beauty to the world. The only way to bring about such a legacy in the lives of children, who become adults, is if these goals are pursued, if learning well is attended to, if the shaping of character is intentional.

We, as parents, cannot depend on someone else or some other institution to shape the destiny and vision of our children. We must own our responsibility before God to invest our lives, to serve in such a way that our goals become reality. Faith, knowledge, wisdom, and moral virtue must be taught, upheld, treasured, and embraced for a lifetime. It is our service to God to be stewards of our children's lives.

Nelson Mandela said, "Education is the most powerful weapon which you can use to change the world."[1]

Education is not about facts or fill-in-the-blank answers to life. True education shapes vision, purpose, the way people live out their lives in their actions and decisions every day.

A wonder-filled education and the process of helping children and adults learn how to think, how to exercise their mental and creative muscle, is a passion of my life. And it is the purpose of this book. Education of a generation of children is of profound importance to the future of the culture. Shaping a heart, mind, and soul determines the soul, conscience, and character of the next generation.

Our brains, wills, and souls are infinitely capable of accessing amazing potential for growth and strength. Yet active engagement and enthusiasm in learning must be cultivated, nurtured, protected so that our students may grow strong over time.

A passive or reductive education, or one in which imagination, self-motivation, stewardship, and engagement are not developed, creates passive human beings who are easily led with propaganda, who just accept what they are told because of a habit of conforming and fitting in.

Foundational Ideas for a Final Encouragement

The night before I turned in this manuscript, I polled my social media audience about what they would like to have included in this book. (Never do that! It is too late once the book has been written.)

Many of the questions focused on the "formula" sort of answers. And many questions I received focused on how to make this easier.

This chapter is a sort of consecration and consolidation of what I have already written, as a final encouragement to you. Let me summarize, as best I can, the foundational ideas I hope you have gleaned.

1. **The vision, character, enthusiasm, integrity, and perseverance *of the mentor*** are the defining power behind the cultivation of a great

education. When the mentor is alive, passionate, and driven to purpose, excellence, generosity of life, then their influence will be contagious. Mentoring through a foundation of love, acceptance, and affection is at the core of the relationship. (Make a plan for yourself to grow and stay encouraged. Read books, listen to podcasts that nurture your vision, that restore your enthusiasm. Attend conferences that add grace and support of your ideals. Meet with friends who are walking the same road. Plan rest, refreshment, restoration along the way.)

2. **Engaging your child's or children's imagination and ability to wonder,** to question, to create, to become involved with the scope and importance of knowledge is the key to their ownership of learning. Understand that active engagement and personal involvement create mental strength and shape a robust love for learning for a lifetime, which is our goal. When you invite their input, they feel more reason to be active and responsive. Plan a more active engagement in learning.

3. **Spiritual formation as a foundation for learning** establishes a philosophical and personal conviction about how to see the world. To grant a pathway to what matters in life, faith in God, the whys of the world, moral excellence, understanding wise ways to live, and the truth that leads to spiritually abundant life are foundational as a background for all that is learned. Walking on the path of life with our children and naturally passing on our spiritual values morning, noon, and night is the optimal way of showing and living an authentic spiritual life. Discipleship requires personal time.

4. **Excellent resources of the best books, writers, artists, musicians, and scientists** provide the first door to developing an appetite for the best food for thought. Resources that provide visual, oral, actual involvement open up wider appetites for wonder to feed upon. Museums filled with artifacts, art, and science and nature

centers as well as concerts should be sprinkled through the years to provide firsthand observation and exploration. Activities and specialized classes, especially in the later years, help broaden first-hand knowledge. Regular exposure to deep and expansive thoughts and engagement in mental wondering prepares the brain to make multiple and valuable connections that increase intelligence and mental muscle.

5. **Determine to refresh your vision, to take time to restore your ideals,** to keep your life ordered and centered on a regular basis. In the marathon of the years of learning, training, and instruction, the differing ages and seasons of life require refreshment and growing knowledge. Developing through input and inspiration helps the formation of more mature minds, thinking skills, and convictions. Create routines and rhythms that make your lifestyle more sustainable and supported. Create a home atmosphere that undergirds your goals and that serves your purposes.

6. **Pass on vision and intentionality for how to live a worthy story.** Provide opportunities to serve, to develop character and resilience as life habits. Cultivate a sense of purpose through the imagination and stewardship of skills, talents, and resources in the pathways of your students. Cultivate in them a confidence to live well-formed lives and to pursue vocations that fit their personalities, drives, skill sets, training, and calls.

This is a very short list. Know that an investment of love, care, guiding into a life of learning, engaging in what matters, cultivating an atmosphere of faith daily is a worthy way to pour out your life.

Yes, there were struggles, doubts, but for the moment. The goal of a stable place in their faith walk with the Lord, an excellently developed life, and the ability to grow in healthy relationships provided a place for growth mentally, spiritually, emotionally, and in self-actualization. I love to hear what my own children are thinking and reading, to grow in my own understanding of life, because they have all surpassed my own knowledge and understanding of life. But the best part is that I had the privilege of laying the foundation of education upon which they built and expanded their adult lives. I found this to be more emotionally gratifying and satisfying than I ever knew it would be. Now I know it was a worthy investment.

> *I see now that while I thought I was shaping them, in reality I was being shaped, taught, and strengthened by my own Father.*

Of course there were challenges along the way. We had to partner with our children through all the pathways of their young adult lives as they pushed against a very secular culture and had to own their beliefs in an adult way.

But I see now that while I thought I was shaping them, in reality I was being shaped, taught, and strengthened by my own Father.

What Would I Change?

Many have asked me what I would change about the ideals we embraced and the journey we made. I would not change any of the learning philosophy of shaping a wonder-filled life. I would have found more joy in the journey. For us, it was a superior way to educate our children. All were able to accomplish what they needed to for college entrance exams and for performing well in university settings as a result of this philosophy, though that was not the goal. So many worry about this, and I think they are focusing on the wrong goals. A rich heart, mind, and soul are the goal, which also secondarily prepares them to perform adequately in the rest of life.

I would have trusted more, fretted less, and put my worries in the file drawer of heaven. As I was trying to figure out the mysterious aspects of my children's challenges in life, I would have accepted by faith that I was the mother he or she needed and that my home would be a place where they would ultimately be able to flourish in their unique life puzzle.

I would have been more at ease in the process and trusted in the goodness of the plan. I would have been more patient with the normal growing stages, as all children have matured from babyhood to adulthood by passing through the natural maturing steps for all of history, every generation.

I would have put less stress on myself and rested more. I would not have entertained so many thoughts of my inadequacies or paid attention to comparison with others. Home is a perfectly adequate place to nurture strong, faithful human beings. And it has been such a place through the centuries.

I wish I had known more experienced parents who had gone before us who could have given us support and encouragement along the way. It is why I do what I do now. I do not wish for anyone to be alone in this process, and I write and speak to try to give hope and encouragement so that others will not feel so alone.

Developing a Strong "Wonder" Muscle Takes Time and Commitment

Time is one of the most essential resources in providing lots of food for wonder so that the muscle of imagination can be exercised and become strong. A lifetime of modeling these values will cost one a laying aside of their own personal goals to invest in those who need direction and focused shaping in order to access their full scope of abilities. Again, it is not about a curriculum, it is about relationship, discussion, engagement, and affirmation that require a dedicated human being to give personal attention.

Overcoming the fear of not being able to check all the boxes or of not covering all the material that the *schools* have suggested is the measure of education requires faith and confidence that says, "I believe the risk I am taking is the right way to steward my child's heart, soul, and mind so that they have the opportunity to grow strong mentally, spiritually, creatively, and emotionally."

Learning to trust a person's natural desire to know, giving honor to unique personalities, drives, and development takes the courage to go against the crowd.

The Cost

Living in the atmosphere of a life of wonder will be messy. There will be paints and play dough, Legos and puzzles, music and stories, hikes in nature that end in storms, discussions, doubts, endless questions. Normal fusses and self-centeredness will be encountered. Weariness and self-doubt can find its way inside our imperfect selves. Much effort and energy go into cultivating independent areas of interest, giving freedom to facilitate the uniqueness of each child.

Home is your garden of life, and you are free to order it and plant it as you will. There must be much planting and arduous cultivating for it to flourish. But all great works of life must be planned in order to make them productive, useful, and flourishing. And all great plans must be worked.

Yes, it is a marathon to raise wholehearted children. Don't compromise your ideals or faith along the way. Pace yourself and keep your eyes on the goal.

Watch Out for Naysayers

I remember when my children were young and I, at age forty-two, had just given birth to Joy, and a relative innocently observed, "You know, sometimes your home looks like it is more of a mess of life than strategic. Don't you think at some point you will have to become a little bit more focused and organized so we can be sure they are learning well?"

These kind of statements that came from many friends, relatives, and neighbors always stabbed me in the insecure corner of my heart. Yet, I would pray, ponder, and recommit to the ideals I believed were making a big difference in my children's hearts, minds, and souls.

When I had a good night of sleep (which was rare) and was granted that magical moment of seeing forward in their lives, I could *almost* see inside their minds, glimpsing a future of flourishing well in their adult lives. Children's growing, deeply engaged minds; highly active curiosity; strong moral convictions; independent thinking skills; relational maturity; love;

and faith cooperate with the way they were designed. I observed that these areas were growing stronger every day, all through the years.

The Risk, Cost, and Commitment Lead to Heartfelt Rewards

I cannot speak for everyone or every story. I am here to share my own story and experience in hopes that something I wrote might encourage or help you in your journey of parenting and teaching. But this path has created for me and for Clay the most rewarding and affirming legacy of our lifetime. I hope it is that way for you.

> *This path has created for me and for Clay the most rewarding and affirming legacy of our lifetime. I hope it is that way for you.*

Such a commitment to live outside the box of expected ways of learning requires resisting the need to have all conform to one standard. It requires choosing to turn away from a fear that suggests that what you are doing is not enough. The choice to resist fitting into a normative, check-off-the-list sort of education where progress can be measured by limited objectives requires confidence and faith on the part of the teacher. Goals must be larger, not just to cover facts, but to inspire hearts, to engage creativity, to employ wonder and imagination, to shape independently strong minds that can evaluate ideas for their real merit, and these goals must be intentionally worked toward.

The gift of wonder will serve children best over their lifetime. Instead of only lecture and textbooks, there will be endless times observing creation and the natural world, pondering human nature and choices made in history, creating a rich thought life instead of just passively entertaining to wile away hours. When we direct a life filled with a vault of intellectual and faith treasures, we provide resources stretching all ages to live into their capacity wherever they find themselves. We provide a royal life.

Even as we observe God as a Father, we see He provided an endless playground of amazing resources to explore. This world is where our curiosity and wonder allow us to uncover and discover the mysteries of science, the mathematic formulas that undergird all the systems of nature, and the joy of creating and subduing the diverse and interesting world in which He placed us. Time and a habit of pondering leads to a better understanding and worship of our creator God.

Not all of the learning will be immediately measurable, but faith in the eyes of one's heart growing strong inside, where we cannot see, will fuel our vision to calculate that a different way of education is worth the investment.

May you find the faith to take the risk and generous love to serve your students, to educate a different way, to trust in the intelligence and capacity already resting inside your child, just waiting to be cultivated and released. And may your own soul become enlightened in the journey.

I pray blessing and favor for each of you as you put the pieces of your own puzzle together and as you shape your own story around wonder abounding. May your life and the lives of your children be wonder-full!

Notes

Chapter 1: A Wonderful Beginning

1. *Oxford Dictionary of English*, third edition, ed. Angus Stevenson (Oxford, England: Oxford University Press, 2010), 2040.

2. C. S. Lewis, *The Weight of Glory: And Other Addresses* (New York: HarperCollins Publishers, 2001), 42.

3. Hoecker, Jay L., "Should I be concerned that my 2-year-old doesn't say many words and is hard to understand?," Mayo Clinic, March 12, 2019, https://www.mayoclinic.org/healthy-lifestyle/infant-and-toddler-health/expert-answers/toddler-speech-development/faq-20057847.

4. Plato, *Theaetetus*, trans. Benjamin Jowett (CreateSpace, 2019), 96.

5. St. Thomas Aquinas, *The Summa Theologica*, trans. Fathers of the English Dominican Province (London: Washbourne, 1914), 385.

6. G. K. Chesterton, *Tremendous Trifles* (New York: Dodd, Mead and Company, 1920), 7.

Chapter 4: Mentoring with Love and Lifegiving Influence

1. The results of one of the most recent studies on this subject can be found in Sandee LaMotte, "MRIs Show Screen Time Linked to Lower Brain Development in Preschoolers," *CNN*, November 4, 2019, https://www.cnn.com/2019/11/04/health/screen-time-lower-brain-development-preschoolers-wellness/index.html.

Chapter 5: Forming Faith through Imagination and Wonder

1. John 13:34; 15:12; 15:17.
2. Matthew 18:22.
3. Matthew 11:29.

Chapter 6: Heartfelt Faith That Never Stops Growing

1. Gerard Manley Hopkins, "As kingfishers catch fire, dragonflies draw flame;" *The Poems of Gerard Manley Hopkins*, fourth edition, eds. W. H. Gardner and N. H. MacKenzie (Oxford, England: Oxford University Press, 1967), 90.

Chapter 9: Creating Wonder-Filled Culture Shapers

1. Andy Crouch, *Culture Making: Recovering Our Creative Calling* (Downers Grove, IL: InterVarsity Press, 2008), 105.

Chapter 10: The Battle and Joy of Shaping a Wonder-Filled Home

1. Sally and Sarah Clarkson, *The Lifegiving Home: Creating a Place of Belonging and Becoming* (Carol Stream, IL: Tyndale Momentum, 2016), 19–20.

2. Joy Clarkson, "About," Wanderings and Ponderings, *JoyClarkson.com,* https://joy clarkson.com/about.

3. Margery Williams, *The Velveteen Rabbit* (Tarrytown, NY: Marshall Cavendish, 2011), 13.

Chapter 11: Securing Wonderful Rhythms, Routines, and Rituals

1. Diana Glyer, "C. S. Lewis, J. R. R. Tolkien, and the Inklings," *C. S. Lewis*, April 16, 2009, https://www.cslewis.com/c-s-lewis-j-r-r-tolkien-and-the-inklings/.

2. C.S. Lewis, *Letters of C.S. Lewis*, revised and enlarged edition, ed. W.H. Lewis (Orlando, FL: Houghton Mifflin Harcourt, 1993), 363.

Chapter 12: Never-Ending Wonder for Lifelong Learning

1. Nelson Mandela, "Nelson Mandela 1918–2013 South African statesman," Oxford Reference, accessed February 27, 2020, https://www.oxfordreference.com/view/10.1093 /acref/9780191843730.001.0001/q-oro-ed5-00007046.

About the Author

SALLY CLARKSON is the bestselling author of more than twenty books, a world-renowned speaker, and a beloved figure who has dedicated her life to supporting and inspiring countless women to live into the story God has for them to tell. She delights in helping others live intimately within the abundant love of God.

Sally has been married to her husband, Clay, for almost forty years, and together they founded and run Whole Heart Ministries, an international ministry seeking to support families in raising faithful, healthy, and loving children in an increasingly difficult culture. Sally also encourages women through her LifewithSally.com membership community and Mom Heart Ministry small groups.

Sally and Clay have four children, Sarah, Joel, Nathan, and Joy, each writers in their own fields as academics, authors, actors, musicians, filmmakers, and speakers.

Sally lives between the mountains of Colorado and the rolling fields of England and can usually be found with a cup of tea in her hands. She loves the companionship of her family, thoughtful books, beautiful music, regular tea times, candlelight, walking, and traveling to see her children.

CLARKSON FAMILY

BOOKS & RESOURCES

Sally Clarkson

- *Seasons of a Mother's Heart*
- *The Mission of Motherhood*
- *The Ministry of Motherhood*
- *Dancing with My Heavenly Father*
- *Desperate* (with Sarah Mae)
- *You Are Loved* (with Angela Perritt)
- *10 Gifts of Heart*
- *Your Mom Walk with God*
- *Own Your Life*
- *The Lifegiving Home* (with Sarah Clarkson)
- *The Lifegiving Table*
- *Different* (with Nathan Clarkson)
- *Only You Can Be You* (with Nathan Clarkson)
- *Girls' Club* (with Joy and Sarah Clarkson)
- *Mom Heart Moments*

Clay Clarkson

- *Educating the WholeHearted Child* (with Sally Clarkson)
- *Our 24 Family Ways*
- *Heartfelt Discipline*
- *Taking Motherhood to Hearts* (with Sally Clarkson)
- *The Lifegiving Parent* (with Sally Clarkson)
- *The Lifegiving Parent Experience* (with Sally Clarkson)

Sarah Clarkson

- *Journeys of Faithfulness*
- *Read for the Heart*
- *Caught Up in a Story*
- *The Lifegiving Home* (with Sally Clarkson)
- *Book Girl*
- *Girls' Club* (with Sally and Joy Clarkson)

Joel Clarkson

- *The Lifegiving Home Experience* (with Sally Clarkson)
- *A Different Kind of Hero* (with Sally Clarkson)
- *The Lifegiving Table Experience* (with Sally and Joy Clarkson)

Nathan Clarkson

- *Different* (with Sally Clarkson)
- *Only You Can Be You* (with Sally Clarkson)
- *Good Man*

Joy Clarkson

- *Own Your Life Experience* (with Sally Clarkson)
- *The Lifegiving Table Experience* (with Sally and Joel Clarkson)
- *Girls' Club* (with Sally and Sarah Clarkson)

Sally Clarkson

AUTHOR | SPEAKER | LIFEGIVER

Beloved author and speaker Sally Clarkson has dedicated her life to the art of mentoring women, encouraging mothers, and educating children. If you would like more daily encouragement in your life from Sally, visit her online at these websites and pages:

WEBSITE & BLOG | SallyClarkson.com

Find daily encouragement for your journey as a woman, mom, and believer on Sally's blog as she shares thoughts, insights, inspiration, wisdom, recipes, traditions, and prayers. You can also stay up to date with her speaking schedule, events, and conferences.

ONLINE COMMUNITY | LifewithSally.com

Life with Sally is an online community of women that was created to reach, teach, and mentor moms worldwide in a more personal way. It is filled with Sally's talks, videos, recipes, Bible studies, workbooks, a forum, and more. It is an online resource to invite a bit of community, wisdom, and joy into today's women's worlds.

PODCAST PAGE | AtHomewithSally.com

Sally invites you into her home and shares personal stories, spiritual insight, and hard-earned wisdom about being a woman, mom, and believer. Filled with dynamic and relevant guests, this podcast, which has been downloaded more than eight million times, will give you a personal and intimate connection into Sally's heart, mind, and home.

Social Media
FACEBOOK | @TheRealSallyClarkson
INSTAGRAM | @Sally.Clarkson
TWITTER | Sally_Clarkson

Whole Heart Ministries

KEEPING FAITH IN THE FAMILY

Whole Heart Ministries is a nonprofit Christian home and parenting ministry founded by Clay and Sally Clarkson in 1994. From the beginning, our mission has been to give help and hope to Christian parents to raise wholehearted children for Christ. Our current strategic ministry initiatives include Sally Clarkson Ministry, Mom Heart Ministry, Storyformed Project, Family Faith Project, Lifegiving Family Project, and WholeHearted Learning. We are keeping faith in the family.

Whole Heart Ministries
PO Box 3445 | Monument, CO 80132
719-488-4466 | 888-488-4466
whm@wholeheart.org | admin@wholeheart.org

For more information, visit our ministry website:
WholeHeart.org